Cooking with All Your Faculties

Menus from Around the World

**Faculty Auxiliary
of the University of Washington**

**Compiled and Edited by
Betty Orians and Sue Christian**

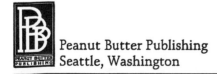

Peanut Butter Publishing
Seattle, Washington

Cover Design: Kelly Pensel
Editors: Sue Christian and Betty Orians
Art Direction: Graphiti Associates, Inc.
Cover Illustration: Karin Kempers
Page Design and Production: Grafisk

Published by Peanut Butter Publishing
200 Second Ave. W.
Seattle, WA 98119
(206) 281-5965

CONTENTS

FOREWORD

What qualifies a long-term politician to write a foreword to such a unique cookbook? Well, I love to eat, and over the years I have had an opportunity to travel to more than 50 countries on five continents. Meals have often been the most memorable experiences of these visits.

Food is a fascinating measure of a society. What people eat and how they prepare their food tell us of their agriculture, history, lifestyle and even their religious beliefs.

Eating in a foreign land is always an adventure. I've learned never to ask about the ingredients until after I have finished the meal. We too often are afraid to try something because it is strange or foreign, or just out of the ordinary. Yet, as a guest, I've always figured that I was being served the best or the most unique of the local dishes. I can't remember ever being disappointed.

So, turn the pages and start experimenting. I know I've already found several fascinating recipes I'd like to try as an enthusiastic but amateur cook. While you're at it, pick up the encyclopedia and learn a little bit more about the country or region from which your recipe comes. Share with your family or guests some of the history, geography and social customs. You'll not only end up with a fine meal, but learn at the same time. That's in the finest tradition of this cookbook sponsored by educators and their families.

Governor Daniel J. Evans

INTRODUCTION

For the past eleven years, it has been my good fortune to be the Honorary President of the Faculty Auxiliary of the University of Washington. I have met and enjoyed many people and admired their dedication to the organization and its goals.

The organization has changed over the years. Originally called the Women's Club, then Faculty Wives, it is now the Faculty Auxiliary and is open to all faculty spouses. The group's goal has always been service to the university community. This includes welcoming newcomers to the campus and providing a way for spouses from all departments to meet and share common experiences.

In 1952, the group began contributing to International Student Aid funds. Since 1957, funds have been raised for full-tuition scholarships. This admirable goal has required many money-making projects, large and small. *Cooking with All Your Faculties* is the latest, and perhaps the most ambitious, of these projects.

This delightful, well-organized cookbook was initiated by the current executive board and named by the current president. Scores of members contributed their prize recipes, their editing and typing skills and their knowledge. It was guided to completion by two stalwart, dedicated members, Sue Christian and Betty Orians. My congratulations to them all.

Here's to much good food, enjoyable gatherings and many student scholarships!

Ruth Gerberding

PREFACE

Faculty Auxiliary is a non-profit organization of the spouses of University of Washington faculty. Its purpose is social, civic and educational. Proceeds from the sale of this book will be used to offer scholarships to students at the University.

In the current spirit of international cooperation, we chose to produce an international cookbook. Our membership provided the ideal base of information. Many members have come here from other countries. Many have had the opportunity to travel widely and to live in other countries. And for many years, Faculty Auxiliary has sponsored an international dinner group, with a strong interest in foods of other lands. *Cooking With All Your Faculties* is a compilation of all this experience.

Our American menu features foods of the Pacific Northwest and a fresh, wholesome cuisine that reflects our lifestyle here.

In planning this book, we had some decisions to make. We decided that we were not writing a basic cookbook: "Grasp handle (small end) of wooden spoon in right hand. . . ." We were not writing the gourmet's compendium: "With a sterling silver spatula, gently fold in $\frac{1}{12}$ teaspoon gnat's eyebrows. . . ."

We have assumed a certain degree of experience in our audience. We came across a cookbook that instructed, "Remove and discard avocado seed." (We were going to stir-fry it?) Another cautioned, "Cut and discard strings from roast." (But we wanted to repair the basketball net.) We haven't included instructions for washing, paring, etc., because we think you have seen the inside of a kitchen before.

Recipes in the book serve 8 to 10, unless otherwise stated. Most ingredients are available in well-stocked supermarkets. Occasionally, we have adapted traditional recipes to Western kitchens.

We have tried to remain non-judgmental about your health. If a recipe called for butter, we called for butter. If you are better off with oil or margarine, you know who you are.

Finally, but most importantly, we offer our sincere thanks to all the people who contributed to the production of this book, in offering recipes and expert consultation, and in offering support services such as editing, marketing and typing.

We also appreciate the patience and support of our husbands,

Gordon Orians and Gary Christian, who listened to constant talk of food by editors who were too busy to cook any of it.

Following is a list of our contributors, without whom we would have a very empty book. Apologies to anyone we have overlooked, because our contact with some contributors was indirect.

Betty Orians

Sue Christian

CONTRIBUTORS

Lorna Aagaard
Nada Aksay
Beata Alden
Dorys Alkire
Helen Aron
Jean Arons
Helen Badgley
Juliet Beard
Josie Bernstein
Tanya Bevan
Carolyn Blunt
Bev Bodansky
Mamie Bolender
Priscilla Bowen
Lucille Boyle
Bonnie Brengelmann
Odile Buchanan
Gail Butterfield
Charlotte Cartwright
Joan Chalk
Mary Clark
Grayce Clay
Molly Cleland
Lillian Crutchfield
Joan Culp
Hady DeJong
Ruth Eller
Eva Ellis
Alberta Ellison
Linda Emery
Beth Etschied
Pat Fischbach
Marianne Fleagle
Eleanor Fordyce
Gay Fridley
Shanta Gangolli
Barbara Garlid
Ruth Gerberding

Gene Geyman
Dennis Glauber
Evette Glauber
Barbara Glicksberg
Edris Glueck
Elaine "Sunnie" Gordon
Margaret Gordon
Charlotte Guebeli
Themis Hadjiioanou
Jane Halver
Barbara Haney
Freda Harris
Sarka Hruby
Martha Hueter
Barbara Jackson
Mari-Ann Jackson
Jessie Johanson
Pam Johnsen
Madelynne Johnson
Ann Jones
Pauline Keiling
Jirair Kevorkian
Seta Kevorkian
Maggie Kimbrough
Bitsy Klee
Cynthia Lair
Caroline Mass
Jill McArthur
Sara McGee
Mary McHugh
Carol McMichael
Theresa Meditch
Jane Mickelson
Claire Mock
Lensey Namioka
Rosemary Newell
Ruth Nilsen
Lydia Nunke

Carol Kittell Oberg
Elaine Phelps
Marie Philipsen
Alice Rasp
Mally Ribe
Carmen Robbin
Ingegerd Roden
Anna Rudd
Andula Ruzicka
Tina Schiess
Melba Schmitz
Ethel Scribner
Arlene Segal
Peg Settles
Pat Shipley
Dulce Sigelmann
Flossie Smith
Yvonne Spadoni
Kay Spelman
Kathleen Stang
JoAnn Stear
Ginney Stevenson
Sheila Swanson

Anita Swarm
Elda Rae Teel
Mary Thomas
Nelda Thompson
Marian Tiffany
Tish Tukey
Margaret Tunks
Vilma Vojta
Mimi Wagar
Fran Waibler
Helen Walker
Barbara Weinstein
Barbara Whittemore
Inga Wilcox
Erica Williams
Kathleen Williams
Naomi Wilson
Polly Wooster
Ann Russell Yeh
Isabella Yen
Nan Yuodelis
Suad Ziadeh

We gratefully acknowledge the following businesses for helping to underwrite the production of this book:

Headlines
Lamont's
QFC
Saxe Floral

ARTISTS

For the illustrations in this book, we approached an introductory drawing class at the University of Washington, under the direction of Professor Spencer Moseley and Teaching Assistant Jackie Mitchell. Each student chose a chapter. The assignment was to create a drawing that would project the "flavor" of the country or the recipes.

The variety of the interpretations and the consistency of the styles was nothing short of amazing. Many thanks to all who participated and whose contributions make this book a unique art study, as well as a useful cookbook.

Jeung-K. Ahn 118, 121
Jean Bhang 80
Sabrina Boler 129, 171
Karen Ness Cate 122, 182, 189
Lisbeth Cavanaugh 10
D.J. Cho 100
Greg Davis 44
Carol Dunn 179
Dothe Foskin 110
Riza D. Gueco 72
Ron Hernandez 18, 148
Jennifer Joyce Johnson 162
Nelly Khoo 26, 32, 35
Tim Lin 104
Kristie Miles 2

Kaja Murphy 156
Thuy Nguyen 41
Greg O'Byrne 64
Kellyjane Paradise 13, 49, 92, 114, 145
Ed Peck 190
Gunars Rauda 172, 174
Scott Riggins 112
J. Harold Saks 165
Jessica Slavin 154
Matt Stafford 38
Luke Stewart 29
Alexis Leigh Vanden Bos 25, 62
Tracy Williamson 5
Dennis Yoon 54

Africa's fascinating cuisines are richer and more varied than most people realize. The recipes here were selected from different countries to illustrate the broad range of cooking.

AFRICA

Tunisian Eggplant Spread

Akara
Nigerian Black-Eyed Pea Balls

Nsima
Malawi Cornmeal Porridge

Caldo de Camarão
Cape Verde Fresh Shrimp Soup

Malawi Ground Nut Chicken

Rice

West African Yam Salad

Central African Republic Spinach Stew

South African Old Cape Brandy Pudding

Tunisian Eggplant Spread

2 large eggplants
3 garlic cloves, cut into 8 slivers each
4 tablespoons extra virgin olive oil, divided
2 cups diced onion
½ cup peeled, seeded and chopped tomato
½ cup seeded and diced green bell pepper
1 teaspoon seeded and minced fresh green hot pepper
⅛ teaspoon cayenne
1 teaspoon ground coriander seeds
¼ teaspoon ground caraway seeds
1 tablespoon cider vinegar
Pinch of curry powder
Salt to taste

Garnish:
Anchovy fillets, rinsed and drained
2 hard-cooked eggs, quartered

Stud eggplants with garlic slivers. Broil on all sides until skin is blistered. Lower heat to 400°F and bake for 35 minutes, or until soft. Cut eggplants in half lengthwise while hot; let drain 10 minutes in a colander. Scrape the flesh from the skin, discarding skin and any hard seeds.

Heat 2 tablespoons oil over low heat; add onion, cover and cook 10 minutes. Add tomato, bell pepper, hot pepper and cayenne; cook over low heat, stirring occasionally for 10 minutes, or until thickened. Remove from heat.

Mash eggplant with a fork until smooth. Fold in onion mixture, coriander, caraway, vinegar, remaining oil, curry powder and salt. Cover and refrigerate until ready to serve.

Garnish with crisscrossed anchovy fillets and egg quarters. Serve with pita wedges.

Akara
Nigerian Black-Eyed Pea Balls

15-ounce can black-eyed peas, drained, liquid reserved
2 eggs
1 small onion, finely chopped
1 small fresh hot pepper, seeded and chopped, or ¼ teaspoon
    cayenne
½ teaspoon salt
Vegetable oil for frying

Wash peas and discard any loose skins that float to the top. Drain. Puree with a few tablespoons reserved liquid in a food processor or blender. Blend in eggs, onion, pepper and salt. If mixture appears dry rather than pasty, add a little more reserved liquid. Beat 2 to 3 minutes, or until light and airy.

Drop by heaping tablespoons into 375°F oil, frying until golden-brown. Test oil temperature with a candy thermometer or by dropping in one spoonful of batter. It should sputter on contact and become golden-brown, without scorching, in about 5 minutes. As the balls are fried, remove with a slotted spoon, and drain on paper towels.

Nsima
Malawi Cornmeal Porridge

By many names and in many versions, this thick porridge is eaten throughout Africa.

1½ cups water
1 tablespoon peanut oil
Salt to taste
½ cup white or yellow cornmeal

Heat water to simmering. Add oil and salt. Pour in cornmeal in a slow, steady stream, stirring for 4 minutes, or until mixture begins to pull away from sides of pot and stick together. Dump into a bowl and shape into a ball. Serve immediately.

Serve in Fresh Shrimp Soup and/or with Ground Nut Chicken. To eat in the traditional manner, tear off a chunk and make an indentation in it with your thumb. Use as an implement to scoop up sauces and stews. You may prefer to put a piece in your bowl of soup.

Caldo de Camarão
Cape Verde Fresh Shrimp Soup

Don't shy away from the shrimp heads; an editor has enjoyed a similar dish at Chez Panisse.

2 green (under-ripe) bananas, peeled and sliced
3 pounds fresh shrimp (unshelled, with heads if possible)
1 teaspoon salt, dissolved in 2 cups boiling water
1 large onion, sliced
2 tablespoons olive oil
3 medium tomatoes, peeled and chopped
2 cloves garlic, minced
1 teaspoon cayenne
4 medium potatoes, peeled and cut in chunks
6 cups water
Nsima (see preceding recipe)

Soak banana pieces in salt water to cover for 10 to 15 minutes to draw out the "pucker" quality of the unripe fruit.

Meanwhile, rinse shrimp in cold, running water. Cook in boiling, salted water for 6 to 8 minutes. Drain, reserving water. Peel and remove heads; press heads through a sieve.

In a pot, saute onion in oil until golden. Stir in tomatoes, garlic and cayenne. Add shrimp, sieved heads, reserved cooking water, potatoes and 6 cups water. Drain bananas and add to pot. Cook 20 minutes, or until everything is tender. This soup is traditionally served with a dollop of *Nsima*.

Malawi Ground Nut Chicken

Ground nuts are peanuts, which grow underground. Ground nut stews are popular throughout Africa.

½ cup flour
½ teaspoon salt
¼ teaspoon pepper
2 (3-pound) chickens, cut into serving pieces
3 tablespoons peanut oil
4 cups finely chopped peanuts
3 cups chicken broth
8 tomatoes, chopped
1 large onion, chopped
2 small hot peppers, seeded and chopped
4 hard-cooked eggs, sliced
2 oranges, peeled and sliced
Hot cooked rice or *Nsima* (see page 6)

Mix flour, salt and pepper; coat chicken. Brown in oil over high heat. Transfer to a 3-quart casserole. Mix peanuts, broth, tomatoes, onion and peppers. Pour over chicken. Cover and bake at 350°F for 1 hour, or until tender. Garnish with sliced eggs and oranges. Serve with rice or *Nsima*, to absorb the sauce.

West African Yam Salad

African yams are different from ours. Our yams are simply a sweeter variety of sweet potato. This salad is delicious made with sweet potatoes or white potatoes.

2 pounds sweet potatoes
6 tablespoons peanut oil
3 tablespoons lemon juice
½ teaspoon salt
¼ teaspoon pepper
1 medium green bell pepper, chopped
1 small onion, chopped
1 rib celery, chopped
3 hard-cooked eggs, peeled and coarsely chopped

Boil sweet potatoes in salted water to cover for 30 to 35 minutes, or until tender; drain. Cool, peel and cube.

Mix oil, lemon juice, salt and pepper; pour over sweet potatoes. Cover and refrigerate at least 4 hours. Stir in green pepper, onion, celery and eggs.

Central African Republic Spinach Stew

1 large onion, finely chopped
2 tablespoons oil
4 tomatoes, peeled and sliced
1 green bell pepper, chopped
3 pounds fresh spinach, chopped; or 4 (10-ounce) packages frozen
1 teaspoon salt
2 small hot peppers, finely chopped, or ½ teaspoon cayenne
6 tablespoons peanut butter

In a large stew pot, saute onions in medium-hot oil until golden. Add tomatoes and green pepper; saute 2 minutes. Add spinach, salt and hot pepper. Cover, reduce heat and simmer 5 minutes.

Thin peanut butter with several tablespoons warm water to make a smooth paste; stir into stew. Continue cooking another 10 to 15 minutes, stirring frequently. Add small amounts of water as necessary to prevent burning.

South African Old Cape Brandy Pudding

This pudding is really a cake in the English tradition.

1 cup dates
1 cup boiling water
1 teaspoon baking soda
½ cup butter
1 cup sugar
2 eggs
1½ cups flour
½ teaspoon salt
¼ teaspoon baking powder
½ cup chopped almonds

Syrup:
1¾ cups sugar
1 cup water
1 tablespoon butter
¾ cup brandy
1 teaspoon vanilla

Combine dates, water and baking soda; set aside to cool completely.

Cream butter and sugar. Beat in eggs. Mix flour, salt, baking powder and almonds. Stir into creamed mixture.

Fold date mixture into batter. Pour into a greased and floured 9 × 13 × 2-inch baking dish and bake at 375°F for 40 minutes, or until cake tests done.

For syrup, boil sugar, water and butter for 5 minutes. Remove from heat and add brandy and vanilla. Prick warm cake all over and pour hot syrup over surface. Let stand several hours. Serve with sweetened whipped cream.

This dinner is likely to be eaten at midday, when the main meal is served. From the Hungarian Liptauer cheese to the excellent coffee, a legacy of the Turks, Austrian cooking reflects the many influences of neighboring countries. This menu wouldn't be complete without a **torte** from the famous dessert capital of the world.

AUSTRIA

Liptauer
Liptauer Cheese

Gefüllte Gurken
Stuffed Cucumbers

Frittaten Suppe
Pancake Soup

Gespickte Kalbsvögerln
Veal Birds

Bramborové Knedlíky
Potato Dumplings

Spinat Nach Wiener Art
Viennese Spinach

Wiener Salat
Viennese Salad

Linzertorte
Linzer Cake

Wiener Kaffee
Viennese Coffee

Liptauer
Liptauer Cheese

8 ounces cream cheese, room temperature (or 1 cup quark*)
½ cup unsalted butter, room temperature
1½ to 2 tablespoons sweet Hungarian paprika
⅛ teaspoon, or less, anchovy paste
1 to 2 tablespoons finely chopped onion

Beat together all ingredients until very smooth. Form into a mound and chill 2 hours until firm. Spread on pumpernickel bread or crackers.

* *Quark is most like the Austrian cheese and is available at health food counters.*

Gefüllte Gurken
Stuffed Cucumbers

3 (7-inch) cucumbers, peeled
1 teaspoon salt
3 sardines, boned, or ⅛ teaspoon anchovy paste
½ cup finely diced cooked ham
3 hard-cooked eggs, chopped
1 green onion, finely chopped
3 tablespoons finely chopped gherkins
1½ teaspoons Dijon mustard
¼ cup mayonnaise

Cut cucumbers in half lengthwise; scoop out seeds. Rub insides with salt and let stand 15 minutes. Wipe dry with a paper towel.

Mash sardines to a paste; add ham, eggs, onion, gherkins, mustard and mayonnaise. Spoon into cucumbers and chill 1 hour.

Before serving, cut each cucumber boat into 4 pieces.

Frittaten Suppe
Pancake Soup

1 cup milk
1 egg
1 cup flour
¼ teaspoon salt
2 tablespoons finely chopped parsley
3 tablespoons butter
3 quarts beef consomme or broth

Beat milk and egg together. Add flour and salt; beat until very smooth. Stir in parsley. Melt 1 teaspoon butter in a crepe pan or nonstick frying pan. When hot and bubbly, pour in a small amount of batter and tip pan to spread uniformly over the bottom. Cook until lightly browned; turn to cook the other side. Repeat until all the batter is used. Roll each pancake and cut into ¼-inch strips.

Heat consomme and add pancake strips. Serve hot.

Gespickte Kalbsvögerln
Veal Birds

3-pound veal round roast, sliced ½ inch thick
¼ pound salt pork or bacon, finely diced
¾ cup fresh fine bread crumbs
1 cup sour cream, divided
1 egg, lightly beaten
2 tablespoons finely chopped parsley
2 teaspoons grated lemon peel
1 clove garlic, minced
½ teaspoon thyme
⅛ teaspoon black pepper
2 medium onions, sliced
4 tablespoons butter
4 carrots, sliced
⅓ to ⅔ cup beef broth

Remove fat from margins of veal slices; dice fat finely. Pound veal slices to ¼ inch thick and cut into pieces about 2 × 4 inches.

Mix diced veal fat and salt pork with bread crumbs. Combine 3 tablespoons sour cream with egg. Add to crumb mixture. Add parsley, lemon peel, garlic, thyme and pepper; mix.

Spread 1 teaspoon mixture in center of each piece of veal. Roll up and tie.

Saute onion in butter until soft and yellow; remove and set aside. Brown veal birds on all sides. Add onion, carrots and ⅓ cup broth. Simmer, covered, for 30 minutes, or until tender, adding more liquid as needed.

Remove veal birds to a warm serving platter and remove strings. Stir remaining sour cream into sauce and heat. Spoon vegetables and sauce over birds.

Bramborové Knedlíky
Potato Dumplings

See recipe on page 42. These dumplings are popular in Austria as well as other Middle European countries.

Spinat Nach Wiener Art
Viennese Spinach

4 (10-ounce) packages frozen chopped spinach, thawed,
    or 3 pounds fresh
5 tablespoons butter
1 small clove garlic, minced
⅓ cup flour
1 cup chicken stock or milk
¼ teaspoon nutmeg
¼ teaspoon salt
⅛ teaspoon pepper

Cook spinach according to package directions, or if using fresh, stem, chop and boil 5 minutes; drain. Puree.

In a saucepan, saute garlic in butter for 1 minute. Add flour and cook, stirring constantly, over low heat for 3 minutes. Stir in pureed spinach and stock. Add nutmeg, salt and pepper; cook 2 minutes longer, stirring constantly.

Wiener Salat
Viennese Salad

Dressing:
¾ cup olive oil
½ cup tarragon or white wine vinegar
½ teaspoon sugar
½ teaspoon paprika
½ teaspoon dry mustard
¼ teaspoon salt
¼ teaspoon pepper

Salad:
3 medium boiling potatoes
3 eggs
3 heads butter lettuce, torn
1 cucumber, peeled and thinly sliced
½ cup finely julienned celery root (celeriac), or thinly sliced celery

Combine dressing ingredients in a jar. Cover and set aside.

Boil potatoes until just tender. Keep warm until ready to assemble and serve salad. Peel and dice at the last minute.

Hard-cook eggs and keep hot. Peel and dice at the last minute.

Toss together lettuce, cucumber, celery root and potatoes with enough dressing to coat lightly. Gently stir in diced eggs. Serve at once.

Linzertorte
Linzer Cake

½ cup butter, room temperature
½ cup sugar
1 egg, room temperature
Grated peel of ½ lemon
½ teaspoon cinnamon
¼ teaspoon salt
⅛ teaspoon cloves
1½ cups flour
1 cup ground hazelnuts or almonds
½ teaspoon baking powder
1 cup raspberry jam

Cream together butter and sugar until fluffy. Beat in egg, lemon peel, cinnamon, salt and cloves. Mix flour, ground nuts and baking powder. Stir into creamed mixture.

Press into a 10-inch springform pan, building a small lip. Fill with jam. Bake at 325°F for 50 minutes, until light brown. Cool 10 minutes on a rack. Remove sides of pan; cool completely. This cake may be served with whipped cream.

Wiener Kaffee
Viennese Coffee

When the Turks were forced to flee Austria in 1683, they left behind sacks of coffee beans, from which the Austrians gained a lasting appreciation of the rich, full-bodied flavor. Today they take their coffee very seriously, brewing it in five distinct forms.

Brazil's national dish of black beans and meat, **feijoada completa**, creates a colorful and festive table for a dinner party. **Feijoada** is served over rice and sprinkled with toasted manioc flour. Sliced oranges, greens and a hot lemon pepper sauce complete the dinner.

BRAZILIAN
FEIJOADA COMPLETA
Complete *Feijoada* Meal

Feijoada
Black Beans and Meats

Farofa
Toasted Manioc Flour

Arroz Brasileiro
Brazilian Rice

Couve à Mineira
Sauteed Collards

Laranjas
Sliced Oranges

Môlho de Pimenta e Limão
Lemon Pepper Sauce

Suspiros
Meringue "Sighs"

Quindins
Coconut Custard Tarts

Batidas
Rum and Lime Cocktails

Cafezinho
Espresso Coffee

Feijoada
Black Beans and Meats

Traditionally, the Brazilians relished the fat from all the meats, but today's health-conscious cooks have found ways to reduce the fat content. This dish is better if prepared a day ahead and reheated.

4 cups (2 pounds) dried black beans
2 ½ quarts water
2 linguiça sausages
¾ pound sausages, Italian or smoked
1 pound pork steaks or chops
2 or 3 smoked ham hocks
1 pound smoked neck bones, beef or pork, optional
1 pound corned beef, rinsed and cut into 4 pieces
12 strips beef jerky
2 tablespoons corn oil
1 large onion, finely minced
6 to 8 green onions, finely minced
½ cup finely chopped parsley
3 drops hot pepper sauce
1 pound cooked tongue, preferably smoked

Wash and pick over beans. Soak overnight in water to cover; drain. Place in an 8-quart pot and add water to cover.

Prick *linguiça* and other sausages. Place on a rack in an oven pan. Add pork, ham hocks and neck bones. Bake at 325°F for 45 minutes to remove excess fat. Set sausages aside.

Add pork, ham hocks, neck bones, corned beef and beef jerky to beans. Cover and simmer 2 hours, or until beans are tender, adding more water as needed. Stir occasionally. Mash 2 cups of the beans to thicken the sauce.

Saute onion in oil until tender. Stir in green onion, parsley and hot pepper sauce. Add to beans. Cook 20 minutes on low heat, stirring so beans don't stick to the bottom of the pot. Remove meats. Reserve corned beef and jerky. Cube pork and remove meat from ham hocks and neck bones; return to beans.

(At this point, you may refrigerate beans and meats for a day to improve the flavor.)

Heat corned beef, jerky, sausages and tongue in a little liquid from the beans. Cut sausages into ½-inch slices; slice corned beef and tongue. Arrange, with beef jerky, on a platter. Reheat beans and serve in a tureen or large bowl.

Farofa
Toasted Manioc Flour

3 slices bacon, diced
1 cup manioc (cassava) flour or farina for hot cereal
1 hard-cooked egg, diced
2 tablespoons sliced black or green olives
1 tablespoon finely chopped parsley

Fry bacon until crisp. Do not drain fat. Remove from heat and gradually add manioc flour. Return to heat and saute until lightly browned. Add egg, olives and parsley. Serve in a small bowl to sprinkle over the *feijoada* at the table.

Arroz Brasileiro
Brazilian Rice

3 tablespoons olive oil
1 large onion, thinly sliced
2 cups long-grain white rice
4 cups boiling water
2 medium tomatoes, coarsely chopped
½ teaspoon salt

Saute onion in oil for 5 minutes. Pour in rice and saute 2 to 3 minutes. Add water, tomatoes and salt; return to a boil, stirring. Reduce heat, cover and simmer 20 minutes, or until rice has absorbed all the moisture. Serve hot.

Couve à Mineira
Sauteed Collards

1 large bunch collards or kale, to make 4 cups when shredded
¼ cup bacon fat or corn oil
Salt and pepper to taste

Remove tough stems from greens. Shred by bunching leaves together and slicing finely. Plunge into boiling water for 3 minutes. Drain well. Gently saute in hot fat until greens are crisp-tender. Add salt and pepper and serve at once.

Laranjas
Sliced Oranges

6 large navel oranges

Peel and remove white pith. Slice oranges crosswise. Arrange on a plate. (May be prepared ahead and refrigerated, covered.)

Môlho de Pimenta e Limão
Lemon Pepper Sauce

3 to 4 preserved *malegueta* or tabasco peppers, drained
½ cup chopped onion
1 clove garlic
½ teaspoon salt
½ cup fresh lemon juice

Puree peppers, onion, garlic and salt. Add lemon juice and let stand just 1 hour. Serve in a small bowl.

Suspiros
Meringue "Sighs"

6 egg whites, room temperature (save yolks for *Quindins*)
¾ teaspoon cream of tartar
⅛ teaspoon salt
1½ cups sugar
1 teaspoon almond or vanilla extract

Beat whites with cream of tartar and salt until peaks form. Add sugar, 1 tablespoon at a time, and continue beating until mixture forms soft, glossy peaks. Mix in extract. Drop rounded teaspoonfuls 2 inches apart onto a foil- or parchment-lined baking sheet. Bake at 250°F for 35 to 45 minutes, until firm and thoroughly dry. Turn off heat and open oven door to allow meringues to cool gradually. Store tightly covered.

Makes about 5 dozen.

Quindins
Coconut Custard Tarts

1¼ cups sugar
6 tablespoons butter, room temperature
6 egg yolks
1 cup flaked coconut
½ teaspoon vanilla

Cream together sugar and butter. Stir in yolks, coconut and vanilla.

Butter twenty 2-inch tartlet pans. Sprinkle lightly with sugar. Divide batter among pans. Set pans in an ovenproof dish and surround with water. Bake at 400°F for 20 to 25 minutes, or until toothpick comes out clean. Loosen edges with a knife and remove while hot. Tarts may be put in small paper or foil cups for serving.

Batidas
Rum and Lime Cocktails

1½ cups fresh lime or lemon juice
1½ cups sugar
3 cups *cachaça* or light rum

Dip rims of 10 glasses first in juice, then in sugar. Combine rum with remaining juice and sugar. Shake with several ice cubes and strain into frosted glasses.

In a traditional Chinese meal, the table is already set with the cold dishes when guests are seated. Soup follows, then stir-fried dishes. Those requiring longer cooking are served last. Desserts are rarely served. These recipes are not as salty as a Chinese cook would make them. The Chinese prefer more salt because of their custom of eating several bowls of plain rice at a meal.

CHINA

Lu Jidan
Eggs in Sauce

Liang Ban Buocai
Spinach Salad

Liang Ban Jisi
Chicken Salad

Cha Shao
Barbecued Pork

Suanla Tang
Hot and Sour Soup

Chao Xiaren
Stir-Fried Prawns

Jiangbao Jiding
Stir-Fried Chicken with Cashews

Guotie
Pot Stickers

Rang Xiangu
Stuffed Mushrooms

Baifan
Rice

Xingren Dofu
Almond Creme

Lu Jidan
Eggs in Sauce

8 to 10 hard-cooked eggs (1 per person)
¼ cup dark soy sauce
1 tablespoon sherry
1 tablespoon sugar
10 sprigs fresh coriander

Peel eggs and place in one layer in a nonreactive saucepan. Add soy sauce, sherry, sugar and enough water to cover the eggs. Simmer until eggs acquire a nice brown color; cool.

To serve, cut each egg in half lengthwise and arrange on individual plates. Garnish with coriander.

This sauce is usually saved for future preparation of other dishes. It becomes richer with each use. In Beijing, people joke that the sauce, used over and over for years, becomes a family heirloom.

Liang Ban Buocai
Spinach Salad

2 (1-pound) bunches spinach, stemmed
1½ tablespoons peanut butter
3 tablespoons water
1½ tablespoons soy sauce
1 tablespoon sesame oil
1 tablespoon sugar

Place spinach in boiling water; when water returns to a boil, cook 30 seconds. Do not overcook. Drain and plunge into cold water. Gently squeeze out water. Slice into 1-inch strips. Arrange on a flat dish.

Mix peanut butter, water, soy sauce, oil and sugar; pour over spinach.

Frozen spinach is not a good substitute for fresh, as its texture is different. Broccoli or asparagus may be substituted for spinach. Peel and cut into small pieces, and parboil until crisp-tender.

Liang Ban Jisi
Chicken Salad

1½ pounds chicken breasts, cut in half
1 tablespoon soy sauce
2 teaspoons dry Chinese mustard
4 ounces rice noodles, broken into 2-inch pieces
¼ cup peanut oil
½ head iceberg lettuce, shredded
½ pound bean sprouts, rinsed
2 tablespoons slivered almonds
2 to 3 green onions, finely chopped

Boil chicken in water to cover for 6 minutes. Remove from heat and let stand 15 minutes. Plunge chicken into ice water; let stand 15 minutes. Drain, pat dry and remove skin and bones. Shred meat.

Mix soy sauce and mustard, adding enough water to make a thin paste. Let stand 15 minutes.

Fry noodles in 2 tablespoons hot oil. Drain on a paper towel. Heat remaining oil and quickly fry the chicken. Remove and cool.

Toss lettuce, sprouts, almonds, onion, noodles and chicken with mustard sauce. Serve immediately.

Cha Shao
Barbecued Pork

2-pound lean pork roast
1 tablespoon soy sauce
1 tablespoon rice wine or sherry
1 tablespoon honey
2 teaspoons sugar
3 cloves garlic, minced
2 tablespoons dry Chinese mustard
¼ cup sesame seeds
Few sprigs fresh coriander

Cut almost through pork along the grain, making a 2-inch wide strip (1). Start the second cut on the opposite side and alternate so end result is one long strip (2). Combine soy sauce, wine, honey, sugar and garlic; rub into pork. Marinate 1 hour.

Spread out pork on a baking sheet and roast at 350°F for 30 minutes. Turn meat and raise temperature to 400°F. Roast 15 minutes longer. Let cool. Slice strips across grain into ¼-inch thick pieces (3). Garnish with fresh coriander.

Mix mustard with enough water to make a thin paste. Let stand 15 minutes.

Serve pork cold with mustard and sesame seeds.

Suanla Tang
Hot and Sour Soup

6 Chinese black mushrooms
12 tree ear mushrooms (lichens)
8 dried day lily flower petals
1 tablespoon peanut oil
¼ cup shredded pork, optional
1 tablespoon light soy sauce
½ cup shredded bamboo shoots
6 cups chicken broth
3 to 4 tablespoons vinegar
1 teaspoon dark soy sauce
2 tablespoons cornstarch
3 tablespoons water
2 cakes pressed *tofu* (soybean curd), cut into strips
1 tablespoon sesame oil
½ teaspoon ground pepper
2 eggs, lightly beaten
1 to 2 tablespoons chopped green onion, for garnish

Soak black mushrooms, tree ears and day lily petals in hot water for 15 to 30 minutes. Discard stems from mushrooms and trim tree ears; slice thinly. Shred day lily petals with fingers (cut off hard end if necessary and slice in half if very long).

Briefly stir-fry pork in hot oil to separate; stir in light soy sauce. Add mushrooms, tree ears, day lily petals and bamboo shoots. Stir-fry 1 minute; add chicken broth. Stir in 3 tablespoons vinegar and dark soy sauce. Taste for seasoning.

Combine cornstarch and water; add to broth. When slightly thickened, add *tofu;* return to a boil. Remove from heat and let stand 30 seconds to let broth cool slightly. Stir in sesame oil and pepper.

Pour soup into a hot pot or tureen; gradually add eggs in a thin stream, stirring constantly. Sprinkle with onion.

Chao Xiaren
Stir-Fried Prawns

1½ pounds prawns, shelled and deveined
2 tablespoons rice wine or sherry
2 tablespoons soy sauce
1 teaspoon cornstarch
1 tablespoon slivered ginger root
2 green onions, sliced
2 tablespoons corn oil
1½ cups frozen peas, defrosted

Marinate prawns in a mixture of wine, soy sauce and cornstarch. Stir-fry ginger and onion in hot oil for 1 minute. Remove prawns from marinade and stir-fry with onion over high heat until pink; stir in marinade. Add peas and stir-fry 2 minutes, or until thoroughly heated.

Jiangbao Jiding
Stir-Fried Chicken with Cashews

5 tablespoons rice wine, divided
5 tablespoons soy sauce, divided
2 tablespoons water
1 tablespoon cornstarch
2 teaspoons sesame oil, divided
1½ pounds boneless, skinned chicken breasts, cut into
    ½-inch cubes
4 tablespoons vegetable oil
1½ cups sliced water chestnuts
3 tablespoons minced green onion
2½ tablespoons minced garlic
2 tablespoons minced ginger root
2 teaspoons chili paste
1½ cups raw cashews, toasted in a 350°F oven until golden

Mix 2½ tablespoons wine, 2 tablespoons soy sauce, water, cornstarch and 1 teaspoon sesame oil. Pour over chicken and marinate at least 20 minutes.

Stir-fry half the chicken mixture in 1 tablespoon hot vegetable oil. Remove. Repeat with other half.

Heat remaining vegetable oil and briefly stir-fry water chestnuts, onion, garlic and ginger. Add chili paste and remaining wine, soy sauce and sesame oil; cook until thick. Add chicken and cashews and stir to coat.

Guotie
Pot Stickers

2½ cups flour
⅔ cup boiling water
⅓ cup cold water
¾ pound Chinese cabbage
¾ pound ground pork
½ cup minced green onion
3 tablespoons soy sauce
1 teaspoon rice wine or dry sherry
1 teaspoon minced fresh ginger root
1 teaspoon sesame oil
6 tablespoons vegetable oil
1⅓ cups water

Garnish:
Fresh coriander sprigs

Dipping sauce:
¼ cup light soy sauce
2 tablespoons rice vinegar or white vinegar
2 teaspoons sesame oil

To prepare dough, place flour in a large bowl. Make a well in the center. Slowly add boiling water, mixing with chopsticks or a fork. Add cold water and mix until smooth. Cover bowl with a damp towel and let stand 15 minutes while preparing filling.

Cook cabbage for 1 minute in boiling water; drain. Plunge into cold water. Drain well, squeezing to remove excess water. Chop blanched cabbage very finely.

Mix pork, onion, soy sauce, wine, ginger and sesame oil. Add cabbage and mix thoroughly. Set aside.

On a floured surface, knead dough until smooth. Divide into 4 pieces. Shape each piece into a roll 12 inches long and cut into 12 pieces. Roll each piece into a ball, pat flat, then roll out to a 2½-inch circle. Cupping a circle in the palm of your hand, place 1 tablespoon filling in center. Firmly pinch edges together over filling to make a seam across the top, forming a crescent.

   In a 12-inch skillet, heat 2 tablespoons vegetable oil over high heat. Place half the dumplings in the skillet without overlapping. Fry 1 minute, or until bottoms are golden. Add ⅔ cup water. Cover and cook until 1 to 2 tablespoons water remain. Add 1 tablespoon vegetable oil to skillet. Simmer, covered, for 1 to 2 minutes. Remove dumplings to a serving platter. Repeat with remaining dumplings.

   Garnish with coriander. Serve hot with dipping sauce, made by combining light soy sauce, vinegar and 2 teaspoons sesame oil.

   Makes 48 dumplings.

Dumplings can be made one day ahead, covered and refrigerated. To reheat, steam for 5 minutes.

Freeze any extras on a baking sheet. Store in a freezer bag. Remove from bag and set dumplings apart to thaw.

Rang Xiangu
Stuffed Mushrooms

24 medium mushrooms

Filling:
6 ounces boneless lean pork
¼ cup drained water chestnuts
3 green onions
½ small hot pepper, seeded
1 teaspoon cornstarch
1 teaspoon grated ginger root
2 teaspoons rice wine or dry sherry
1 teaspoon soy sauce
½ teaspoon *hoisin* sauce
1 egg white

Batter:
½ cup cornstarch
½ cup flour
1½ teaspoons baking powder
½ teaspoon salt
⅓ cup milk
⅓ cup water
Flour for coating
3 cups peanut oil

Remove mushroom stems and finely chop them, along with pork, water chestnuts, onions and pepper; mix together.

Combine cornstarch, ginger, wine, soy sauce, *hoisin* sauce and egg white. Stir into pork mixture. Mound firmly into cavities of mushroom caps.

To prepare batter, combine cornstarch, flour, baking powder and salt. Stir in milk and water.

Coat mushrooms with flour, then batter. Fry a few mushrooms at a time in hot (375°F) oil for 5 minutes, or until golden. Drain on paper towels.

Baifan
Rice

3 cups rice (a mixture of short and long grains gives the best
    flavor and texture)
Cold water to reach 1 inch above surface of rice

Wash rice well in a strainer under running water. Combine with water in a 3-quart heavy saucepan. Cover, bring to a boil over high heat and cook 5 minutes, stirring occasionally. Reduce heat as low as possible and simmer, covered, for 20 minutes. Do not lift cover until ready to serve.

Xingren Dofu
Almond Creme

2 envelopes (2 tablespoons) unflavored gelatin
½ cup cold water
1 quart milk
½ cup sugar
2 teaspoons almond extract
1 teaspoon vanilla
2 cups fresh sliced strawberries, honeydew melon or cantaloupe,
    or canned peaches or lychees

Soften gelatin in cold water. Scald milk. Add sugar and gelatin; stir until gelatin dissolves. Stir almond extract and vanilla into gelatin mixture. Pour into 1½-quart mold. Refrigerate 4 hours, or until set.

Unmold by dipping into hot water for a few seconds. Run a knife around the edge; invert onto a serving plate. Decorate with fruits in season or canned fruits.

Czechoslovakia is a country of two nations, Czechs and Slovaks. The food is robust and satisfying, and reflects the country's geographical position in the center of Europe. The Czechs have transformed dishes from their western neighbors into a cuisine of their own. Slovak cooking is a little spicier, reflecting the influence of Hungary to the southeast. This menu offers samples from excellent cooks of both regions.

CZECHOSLOVAKIA

Rosol Po Česku
Layered Aspic Mold

Segedinsky Gulaš
Sauerkraut Goulash

Bramborové Knedlíky
Potato Dumplings

Chleb
Rye Bread

Čalamáda
Marinated Pepper Salad

Švestkový a Broskvový Koláč
Sabka's Plum-Peach Cake

Rosol Po Česku
Layered Aspic Mold

Make this the day before you plan to serve it.

1 envelope (1 tablespoon) unflavored gelatin
¼ cup dry white wine
1½ cups clear chicken stock
¼ cup cider vinegar
½ teaspoon Worcestershire sauce
1 teaspoon sugar
1 teaspoon salt
¼ teaspoon white pepper
½ cup diced carrots, parboiled and drained
½ cup peas, parboiled and drained
1 cup diced cooked ham
⅔ cup chopped dill pickle
1 small onion, chopped
1 apple, diced
Lettuce leaves

Sprinkle gelatin on wine. Let stand 5 minutes. Heat stock, vinegar and Worcestershire. Add gelatin mixture, sugar, salt and pepper; stir until gelatin dissolves. Pour gelatin mixture 1 inch deep in a lightly oiled 6-cup mold. Chill until firm.

Arrange carrots and peas on chilled layer and pour more gelatin over just to cover. (Warm slightly if too firm to pour.) Chill again until second layer jells. Distribute ham, pickle, onion and apple over second layer and cover with remaining gelatin. Chill overnight.

To unmold, dip mold in hot water for a few seconds.and run a knife around inside of mold. Invert a serving plate over mold and, holding mold and plate together, quickly turn over to release aspic onto plate. Slice and serve on lettuce leaves as a first course.

Segedinsky Gulaš
Sauerkraut Goulash

6 strips bacon, diced
3 pounds pork, not too lean, cut in 1-inch cubes
3 large onions, chopped
2 cloves garlic, minced
1 tablespoon flour
2 pounds sauerkraut, rinsed
1 apple, peeled and grated
1 tablespoon sweet paprika
1 tablespoon caraway seeds
1 teaspoon salt
2 cups water or white wine
1 pound *Kielbasa* (Polish sausage), cut in 1-inch lengths
½ cup sour cream

Brown bacon in a 5-quart pot; remove and set aside. Brown pork in bacon drippings; remove and set aside. Saute onion and garlic in drippings until lightly browned. Stir in flour. Add sauerkraut, apple, bacon, pork, paprika, caraway, salt and water or wine. Cover and simmer 1 hour. Add more water as needed to prevent drying out. Add *Kielbasa* and simmer 20 minutes longer. Add more paprika if necessary to give the goulash a reddish color. Stir in sour cream and serve.

This dish is even better reheated and served a day or two later.

Bramborové Knedlíky
Potato Dumplings

6 medium potatoes
2 eggs, lightly beaten
1½ teaspoons salt
½ cup flour
1 slice white bread, crust removed, cut in cubes
4 tablespoons butter, divided
Flour for coating
½ cup chopped parsley

Boil potatoes in their skins for 30 minutes, or until tender. Chill 12 hours or longer. Peel and mash. Add eggs, salt and flour. Beat until fluffy.

Saute bread cubes in 2 tablespoons butter. Form potato mixture into 1-inch balls with a bread cube in the middle of each.

Roll balls in flour. Drop a few at a time into 2 quarts boiling salted water. When dumplings rise to the surface, cover pot and simmer 8 minutes. Remove with slotted spoon and drain on paper towels. Keep hot. When ready to serve, melt remaining butter and drizzle over dumplings. Sprinkle with parsley.

Čalamáda
Marinated Pepper Salad

1 green bell pepper
1 red bell pepper
1 yellow bell pepper
¾ cup salad oil
¼ cup vinegar
½ teaspoon salt
⅛ teaspoon pepper
1 clove garlic, halved

Seed peppers and slice very thinly. Mix oil, vinegar, salt and pepper. Toss peppers and garlic with dressing and marinate at least 2 hours, stirring occasionally. Discard garlic before serving.

Švestkový a Broskvový Koláč
Sabka's Plum-Peach Cake

¼ pound butter, room temperature
½ cup sugar
2 eggs
Grated peel of 1 lemon
1 cup flour
1 package yeast, softened in ¼ cup warm water (120° to 130°F)
6 to 8 plums, sliced
2 or 3 peaches, sliced
½ cup chopped walnuts
½ cup sugar
½ teaspoon cinnamon

Cream butter and sugar. Beat in eggs and lemon peel. Stir in flour and yeast mixture. Spread in greased 9 × 13-inch pan. Arrange fruit in rows over dough. Sprinkle with nuts.

Set pan in warm (less than 200°F) oven and let cake rise until double. Turn oven up to 350°F and bake for 20 to 25 minutes, until top is lightly browned. Mix sugar and cinnamon; sprinkle over cake. Best served warm. May be frozen and, when thawed, warmed in oven.

The rising middle classes of industrial England made 19th-century feasts more common. They depended on several waiters serving the dishes of each course around the table to each guest in turn. The first waiter might come around with meat, the second with potatoes, the third with a vegetable and the fourth with a sauce. Fifty dishes could be served in one evening.

ENGLAND
A VICTORIAN FEAST

Apéritif
Sherry

Hors d'Oeuvre
Stilton-Stuffed Pears

Soup
Cream of Carrot Soup

Fish
Dressed Crab

Main Meat
Ham in Crust with Vegetables

Ice
White Wine Sherbet

Game
Honey-Glazed Duck

Vegetable
Brussels Sprouts and Chestnuts

Pudding
Second Chance Trifle

Savoury
Mushroom-Anchovy Toast

Dessert
Baked Apples

Coffee   **Port**   **Tea**

Stilton-Stuffed Pears

½ pound Stilton cheese, room temperature
¼ cup butter, room temperature
2 tablespoons heavy cream
⅓ cup chopped walnuts
4 or 5 ripe pears (½ per person)
Juice of 1 lemon
8 to 10 walnut halves

Cream together cheese, butter and cream. Stir in chopped walnuts. Halve and core pears, making a depression to hold 2 tablespoons filling. Brush lemon juice on exposed cut surfaces. Mound Stilton mixture in depression and top with walnut half. Serve within 1 hour. Refrigerate if not served immediately.

Cream of Carrot Soup

2 tablespoons butter
½ medium onion, chopped
1 pound (8 to10) carrots, sliced
1 pound (3 to 5) potatoes, peeled and diced
6 cups rich chicken broth
2 sprigs fresh thyme, or ½ teaspoon dried
1 bay leaf
2 cups half-and-half
½ teaspoon Worcestershire sauce
½ teaspoon sugar
Dash of Tabasco sauce
Salt and white pepper to taste

In a stock pot, briefly saute onion, carrots and potatoes in butter. Add broth, thyme and bay leaf. Cover and simmer 30 minutes, or until vegetables are tender. Remove bay leaf. Puree in food processor or blender. Return soup to pot and bring to a gentle boil. Add half-and-half, Worcestershire, sugar, Tabasco, salt and pepper. Serve hot.

Dressed Crab

5 tablespoons salad oil
3 tablespoons cider vinegar
1 tablespoon dry mustard, divided
2 pounds crabmeat
3 tablespoons chopped parsley
8 to 10 lettuce leaves
1 teaspoon water
½ cup mayonnaise

Mix oil, vinegar and half the mustard. Blend with crabmeat and parsley. Chill.

Arrange lettuce on salad plates and divide crab mixture among them.

Mix water and remaining mustard. Let sit 5 minutes for flavor to develop; add to mayonnaise. Spoon over crab.

Ham in Crust with Vegetables

3- to 4-pound boneless ham
1 tablespoon butter
1 tablespoon oil
3 carrots, finely chopped
2 celery ribs, finely chopped
1 parsnip, finely chopped
1 onion, finely chopped
½ cup port
¼ cup brown sugar
1 teaspoon dry mustard
¼ teaspoon cayenne
¼ teaspoon nutmeg
¼ teaspoon cloves
1 pound frozen puff pastry sheets, thawed
1 egg yolk, whisked with ½ teaspoon water (egg wash)

Remove most of fat from ham. Heat butter and oil in a large nonreactive pot. Saute carrots, celery, parsnip and onion until soft. Add port and ham. Cover and simmer 1 hour. Cool to room temperature. Remove ham and place in a baking dish. Reserve vegetables.

Mix brown sugar, mustard, cayenne, nutmeg and cloves. Rub over ham.

Roll out puff pastry large enough to cover top and sides of ham. Let rest 10 minutes in a cool place. Roll dough around a floured rolling pin; unroll over ham, molding it to the ham. (The crust will not cover the bottom of the ham.) Cut leftover pastry scraps into decorative shapes and attach to crust with egg wash. Brush top of crust with remaining egg wash. Bake at 375°F for 25 minutes, or until crust is golden-brown.

Reheat vegetables to accompany ham.

Carefully remove crust. Slice ham, keeping slices in place. Replace crust over ham. Serve a piece of crust with each ham slice.

Unlike this delicious crust, the traditional crust was not meant to be eaten. It served only as a container to seal the juices in the meat and make a beautiful presentation at the table.

White Wine Sherbet

1 tablespoon gelatin
1¼ cups water, divided
1 cup sugar
2 cups chilled dry white wine
1 cup fresh lemon juice
1 egg white

Soften gelatin in ¼ cup cold water. Over low heat, gently boil sugar and 1 cup water for 10 minutes. Add softened gelatin and stir until dissolved. Chill.

Add wine and lemon juice. Beat egg white until stiff, but not dry. Fold into cold mixture. Spoon into a flat container and freeze until slushy. Stir, freeze 30 minutes and stir again. Freeze until 20 minutes before serving.

Serve in chilled glasses.

Honey-Glazed Duck

This must marinate at least 24 hours before cooking.

2 (4½-pound) ducks, rinsed well and dried
½ cup sherry
1 tablespoon salt
2 teaspoons thyme
2 teaspoons ginger
½ cup honey
½ cup water

Remove excess fat from ducks. Rub inside and out with mixture of sherry, salt, thyme and ginger. Refrigerate 12 hours, breast-side down.

Brush ducks with honey. Refrigerate, breast-side up, overnight or until ready to cook.

Place ducks, breast-side up, on a rack in a roasting pan. Add water. Roast at 400°F for 15 minutes. Lower heat to 350°F and roast 1 hour, or until ducks are tender and drumsticks move easily.

Remove ducks to a serving dish and keep warm. Remove fat and strain. Boil until liquid is slightly thickened. Pour over ducks and serve.

Brussels Sprouts and Chestnuts

¾ pound chestnuts
1 tablespoon sugar
4 tablespoons butter, divided
1 cup chicken broth
2 pounds Brussels sprouts
Pinch of grated nutmeg

Make two cross-cut gashes on the flat side of each chestnut with a sharp knife. Boil in water to cover for 20 minutes. Remove from water and peel.

Heat sugar with 3 tablespoons butter until sugar caramelizes. Add chestnuts and saute until well coated. Add broth and boil 10 minutes or until broth is syrupy.

Trim Brussels sprouts and boil in water to cover for 10 minutes, or until just tender; drain. Add sprouts to hot chestnuts; add remaining butter and nutmeg. Serve hot.

Second Chance Trifle

Trifles are like fingerprints; no two are alike. Trifle was the English cook's ingenious way of using what was on hand to make a new and delicious dessert of yesterday's stale cake. One of our members baked a spice-nut cake for a company dinner. Shortly before the guests arrived, she dropped the cake and it broke into a hundred pieces. Perfect, she thought, for a trifle. Her resourcefulness paid off; her dessert was the hit of the evening!

2½ cups milk, divided
3 tablespoons sugar
1½ tablespoons cornstarch
3 egg yolks
1 teaspoon vanilla
1 un-iced cake, broken into chunks (for example, spice cake, nut
    cake, banana cake or pound cake; slightly stale is fine)
¼ cup kirsch, sherry or brandy
¼ cup raspberry jam, warmed
2 cups fresh raspberries
1 cup heavy cream, whipped

In a saucepan, whisk together ¼ cup milk, sugar, cornstarch and egg yolks. Over medium heat, continue whisking and slowly add remaining milk. When thickened, remove from heat and stir in vanilla. Let cool.

Arrange half the cake pieces in a deep glass bowl. Sprinkle cake with 2 tablespoons kirsch and drizzle with 2 tablespoons jam. Spread half the cooled custard over the cake pieces. Top with 1 cup raspberries.

Repeat with another layer of cake, kirsch, jam, custard and fruit, reserving a few berries for garnish. Top with whipped cream and the reserved berries.

Variations: Substitute blueberries, kiwis or strawberries for raspberries. Use a jam and liqueur that will complement your choice of fruit.

Mushroom-Anchovy Toast

1 small can anchovy fillets
8 to 10 medium mushrooms
¼ cup butter
8 to 10 slices white bread
2 teaspoons stone-ground mustard
¼ cup unsweetened whipped cream, slightly chilled

Drain anchovies and chop finely. Slice mushrooms and lightly saute in 2 tablespoons butter.

Cut bread into 3-inch circles and toast. Spread with remaining butter and a very small amount of mustard. Sprinkle anchovies on toasted circles and arrange mushroom slices on each. Put a teaspoon of whipped cream in the center of each hot toast. Serve immediately.

Baked Apples

4 or 5 large Granny Smith apples
1 orange, grated peel and juice
2 tablespoons orange-flower water
½ cup sugar
2 cups cream

Cut apples in half horizontally and core each all the way through. Arrange cut side down in a baking dish. Put orange peel in the cavities. Mix orange juice and flower water; pour over apples. Sprinkle with sugar.

Bake at 400°F for 25 minutes, adding more juice if apples become too dry. Serve hot or cold with cream.

French cuisine is so varied that a tourist could spend a year or two visiting bistros throughout the provinces, sampling their Sunday chicken and enjoying a very different dish each week. Eating is a sacred ritual, designed to maintain friendships and to put life into perspective.

FRANCE

Mousse de Foies de Volaille
Brandied Chicken Liver Paté with Prunes

Pâté de Champignon
Mushroom Paté

Soupe à l'Oignon
Onion Soup

Sorbet

Suprêmes de Volaille Véronique
Chicken Breasts with Green Grapes

Fenouil Vinaigrette
Fennel with Mustard Vinaigrette

Salade Romaine à la Crème
Romaine Salad with Cream

Gâteau au Chocolat, Noisettes et Grand Marnier
Chocolate Hazelnut Cake with Grand Marnier

Café
Coffee

Mousse de Foies de Volaille
Brandied Chicken Liver Paté with Prunes

The prunes nestled in the paté visually remind the connoisseur of the endangered truffle. The unique addition of the prune flavor stands on its own.

2 medium onions, chopped
1 clove garlic, minced
¾ cup butter, divided
1 pound fresh chicken livers
1 tablespoon flour
1 teaspoon salt
½ teaspoon pepper
1 bay leaf
⅛ teaspoon thyme
⅛ teaspoon oregano
⅛ teaspoon tarragon
3 tablespoons brandy or cognac
6 pitted prunes, simmered in water to cover for 10 minutes,
    or until softened

Saute onion and garlic in ½ cup butter until tender; remove from skillet. Saute livers in ¼ cup butter until pink. Sprinkle with flour and add salt, pepper, bay leaf, thyme, oregano and tarragon. Cover and simmer over low heat for 2 minutes, or until livers are cooked. Discard bay leaf. Combine with onions.

Add brandy and puree in a food processor or blender. Spoon half into a lightly oiled 4½ × 8½ × 2½-inch loaf pan lined with plastic wrap, packing firmly to eliminate air bubbles. Press the prunes lengthwise down the center. Pack remaining mousse on top.

Cover with plastic wrap and refrigerate at least 3 hours, or until firm. Unmold and slice. Serve as a first course along with a slice of mushroom paté (see page 57), garnished with parsley and baby gherkins.

Recipe may be made up to 2 days ahead.

Pâté de Champignon
Mushroom Paté

1 pound fresh mushrooms, sliced
¾ cup butter, divided
1 tablespoon lemon juice
⅛ teaspoon cayenne
2 eggs, scrambled in 1 teaspoon butter
4 tablespoons grated Parmesan cheese
¼ teaspoon tarragon vinegar
½ teaspoon freshly cracked black pepper

Saute mushrooms in ¼ cup butter until limp. Add lemon juice and cook 5 minutes, shaking pan often. Puree in a food processor or blender; cool slightly. Add cayenne, ½ cup softened butter, eggs, cheese, vinegar and pepper. Mix well.

Put in a greased loaf pan and refrigerate at least 2 hours. Unmold, slice and serve on a plate, garnished with parsley and baby gherkins. Accompany with thinly sliced French bread.

Recipe may be made up to 3 days ahead.

Soupe à l'Oignon
Onion Soup

2 tablespoons unsalted butter
¼ cup olive oil, divided
4 cups sliced yellow onions
2 cloves garlic, minced
3 tablespoons flour
3 quarts rich beef stock
1 cup dry white wine
Salt and freshly ground black pepper to taste
8 to 10 slices French bread
2 cups (6 ounces) shredded Gruyère cheese
1¼ cups (4 ounces) freshly grated Parmesan cheese

Heat butter and 2 tablespoons oil over medium-low heat in a large pot. Add onions and garlic; saute 30 to 45 minutes, or until golden. Sprinkle flour over onions and stir. Gradually stir in stock and wine. Season with salt and pepper. Simmer, covered, over low heat for 1 hour.

With remaining oil, brush one side of bread slices. Lay slices on a baking sheet and toast, oil side up, at 350°F for 10 to 12 minutes, or until golden brown.

Preheat broiler. Ladle soup into ovenproof soup bowls. Float a bread slice, toasted side up, in each bowl. Top each slice generously with Gruyère, then with Parmesan. Broil 6 inches from heat for 5 minutes, or until cheese is melted and bubbly. Serve immediately.

Sorbet

Start at least 1 day before serving.

¾ cup sugar, divided
½ cup fresh lemon juice
Peel of 1 orange, finely grated
2 cups water
4 egg whites

Combine ½ cup sugar, lemon juice, orange peel and water. Stir until sugar is completely dissolved; place in freezer. When slightly frozen, beat to a consistency of slush, cover surface with plastic wrap, and refreeze.

When mixture is well frozen, beat egg whites on high speed, gradually sprinkling in remaining ¼ cup sugar, one tablespoon at a time. Continue beating until egg whites hold stiff peaks.

Beat frozen mixture until slushy. Fold in egg whites. Place in a 9 × 13 × 2-inch baking dish, cover with plastic wrap and freeze for 2 hours, or until firm.

Suprêmes de Volaille Véronique
Chicken Breasts with Green Grapes

The name "véronique" usually indicates grapes are part of a dish. Briefly heated, the grapes develop a jewel-like sparkle.

5 large whole chicken breasts, about 5 pounds total
Salt
2 tablespoons butter
1½ tablespoons orange marmalade
½ teaspoon tarragon
½ cup dry white wine
½ cup whipping cream
2 teaspoons cornstarch
2 teaspoons water
1½ cups seedless green grapes

Bone, skin and halve chicken breasts. Sprinkle lightly with salt. Saute in butter for 10 minutes, or until lightly browned on each side. Remove from skillet.

Stir in marmalade, tarragon and wine; bring to a boil. Replace chicken. Reduce heat, cover and simmer gently for 15 minutes, or until chicken is white in the thickest part.

Transfer chicken to a serving dish and keep hot. Add whipping cream to pan juices and bring to a rolling boil over high heat. Blend together cornstarch and water; stir into boiling sauce. Continue boiling until sauce thickens slightly. Add grapes to sauce and quickly return to boiling. Pour over chicken and serve at once.

Fenouil Vinaigrette
Fennel with Mustard Vinaigrette

2 heads fennel (sweet anise)
½ cup white wine vinegar
¼ cup olive oil
2 tablespoons minced shallot
1 tablespoon Dijon mustard
1 teaspoon thyme

Cut woody stems from fennel. Cut each head vertically into ½-inch slices. Place in a baking dish.

Whisk together vinegar, oil, shallots, mustard and thyme. Brush lightly over fennel. Cover and microwave 12 minutes, or until barely tender.

For a barbeque variation, cut each head vertically into quarters. Marinate 20 minutes in dressing. Grill 4 to 6 inches over medium-hot coals, turning frequently, for 15 minutes, or until barely tender.

Salade Romaine à la Crème
Romaine Salad with Cream

⅓ cup heavy cream
2½ tablespoons cream cheese, room temperature
1½ tablespoons lemon juice
Salt and white pepper to taste
1 large head Romaine lettuce, torn

With a fork, combine cream, cream cheese and lemon juice until smooth. Add salt and pepper. Toss with lettuce and serve.

*In 1534, Pope Paul III presented to Rabelais some seeds from lettuce cultivated in the Papal garden in Rome. They were christened "**laitue romaine**," or Roman lettuce, in honor of their origin.*

Gâteau au Chocolat, Noisettes et Grand Marnier
Chocolate Hazelnut Cake with Grand Marnier

¾ pound semi-sweet chocolate
¼ cup water
Juice of 1 orange, or ⅔ cup orange juice
1½ cups softened butter
3 tablespoons sugar
3 egg yolks
1 cup finely ground hazelnuts
¼ cup Grand Marnier liqueur
Grated peel of 1 orange
3 egg whites
½ cup coarsely chopped hazelnuts
18 *Petit Beurre* biscuits, coarsely chopped*
1 cup heavy cream, whipped with 2 tablespoons Grand Marnier

Melt chocolate with water and orange juice in a double boiler. Let cool to room temperature.

Cream butter and sugar. Beat in egg yolks, one at a time. Blend in ground nuts, Grand Marnier, orange peel and cooled chocolate mixture.

Beat egg whites until soft peaks form. Fold into chocolate mixture. Fold in chopped nuts and biscuit pieces.

Line a 4½ × 8½ × 2½-inch loaf pan with plastic wrap, extending the edges an inch beyond the rim. Spoon mixture into loaf pan and chill overnight. Unmold and let stand at room temperature for 30 minutes before serving. Slice and serve with Grand Marnier-flavored whipped cream.

* ***Petit Beurre*** *biscuits can be found in the cookie section of grocery stores. Other butter wafers may be substituted.*

Greg O'Byrne

Where would Greek cooking be without olives? Shops offer a dozen kinds of olives. The choices of olive oils rival the variety of wines. This menu is fit for the gods — and in fact is scheduled for the next banquet on Mt. Olympus.

GREECE

Gemista Media
Stuffed Mussels

Greek Olives and Feta

Tomates Gemistes me Melitzana
Tomatoes Filled with Eggplant

Psito Arnaki
Herb-Stuffed Lamb Roast

Spanakopetakia
Cheese-Spinach Triangles

Sparangia me Avgolemono
Asparagus with Egg-Lemon Sauce

Galaktoboureko
Custard Pastry

Kafes
Greek Coffee

Gemista Media
Stuffed Mussels

30 mussels, cleaned with stiff brush
8-ounce bottle clam juice, divided
¼ cup olive oil
½ cup chopped onion
½ cup long-grain white rice
½ cup pine nuts
¼ cup dried currants
½ cup white wine
¼ teaspoon pepper
3 tablespoons chopped parsley, divided
Lemon wedges for garnish

In a large saucepan, bring ½ cup clam juice to a boil. Add mussels and cook 3 to 5 minutes, or just until shells open; drain. Reserve liquid and strain. Arrange mussels in a single layer in a shallow baking dish. Discard top shells and any that do not open.

Saute onion in oil until golden. Add rice and nuts. Saute until nuts turn golden. Add remaining clam juice, reserved liquid from mussels, currants, wine and pepper. Bring to a boil; reduce heat, cover and simmer 20 minutes, or until all liquid is absorbed. Remove from heat.

Stir in 2 tablespoons parsley. Place 1 tablespoon mixture on top of each mussel in its shell. (Mussels may be prepared several hours ahead and refrigerated until just before serving.)

Bake uncovered at 400°F for 10 minutes, or until hot. Garnish with remaining parsley and lemon wedges. Serve hot or at room temperature.

Tomates Gemistes me Melitzana
Tomatoes Filled with Eggplant

10 tomatoes
1 tablespoon salt
1 medium eggplant, peeled and cubed
1 cup flour
½ cup vegetable oil
½ cup rice
4 teaspoons minced onion
¼ teaspoon pepper
½ cup dry bread crumbs
½ cup coarsely crumbled feta cheese
4 tablespoons minced parsley

Slice tops off tomatoes and set aside. Scoop out pulp, chop, drain and set aside. Salt insides of tomatoes and invert to drain.

Immerse eggplant cubes in cold water as you cut them. When ready to cook, dry with paper towels; roll in flour and fry in oil until golden. Remove and drain on paper towels. Saute rice and onion in the same oil for 5 minutes. Season with pepper, add tomato pulp and simmer 5 minutes. Combine with eggplant, bread crumbs, feta and parsley.

Stuff tomatoes with eggplant mixture; place in a baking dish and replace the tomato tops. Drizzle oil from skillet over tomatoes and bake at 350°F for 25 minutes, or until rice is tender. Serve warm or at room temperature.

Psito Arnaki
Herb-Stuffed Lamb Roast

¾ cup chopped onion
2 to 4 cloves garlic, minced
¼ cup olive oil
2 eggs, beaten
10-ounce package frozen chopped spinach, thawed
¼ cup chopped parsley
3 tablespoons chopped fresh basil, or 1 tablespoon dried
1 tablespoon chopped fresh mint leaves, or 1 teaspoon dried
2 teaspoons crushed fresh oregano, or 1 teaspoon dried
¼ teaspoon pepper
6 cups unseasoned croutons
½ cup water
1 leg of lamb (about 6 pounds), boned and butterflied
1 teaspoon fresh rosemary, or ½ teaspoon dried

Saute onion and garlic in oil until tender but not brown. In a large bowl, combine eggs, spinach, parsley, basil, mint, oregano and pepper. Add onion mixture. Stir in croutons. Drizzle with water to moisten, tossing lightly. Set aside.

Remove fell (pink, paper-thin layer) from surface of lamb. Pound lamb to an even thickness and sprinkle with rosemary. Spread stuffing over roast. Roll up and tie securely. Place roast, seam-side down, on a rack in a shallow roasting pan. Insert meat thermometer in thickest portion of meat. Roast uncovered at 325°F for 1½ to 2 hours, or until thermometer registers 150°F (medium rare). Let stand 15 minutes before carving. Remove strings. Garnish with sprigs of fresh herbs.

Spanakopetakia
Cheese-Spinach Triangles

5 tablespoons olive oil, divided
½ cup finely chopped onion
2 tablespoons finely chopped parsley
1½ teaspoon dill weed
¾ pound fresh spinach, stemmed and chopped
1½ teaspoons flour
⅛ teaspoon pepper
1 egg, lightly beaten
¾ cup crumbled feta cheese
¾ cup butter
12 sheets (about ½ pound) *filo* dough

Saute onion, parsley and dill in 3 tablespoons oil until soft. Add spinach and saute until moisture has evaporated. Stir in flour and pepper; let cool. Combine egg and cheese; stir into spinach mixture. Set filling aside.

Melt butter and 2 tablespoons oil together. Remove one *filo* sheet at a time. Keep remaining sheets covered with plastic wrap and a damp cloth to prevent drying. Brush lightly with butter mixture, and cut crosswise into thirds. Fold each strip lengthwise into thirds.

Spread 1 teaspoon filling on corner and fold corner over to form triangle. Continue folding strip in triangles down the full length to make one multi-layered triangle. Repeat with remaining *filo* and filling.

Arrange triangles on a buttered baking sheet. Brush lightly with butter mixture. Bake at 350°F for 25 minutes, or until golden. Serve warm.

Makes 3 dozen.

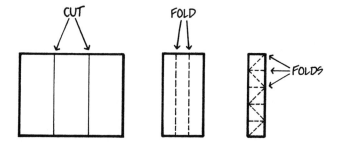

Sparangia me Avgolemono
Asparagus with Egg-Lemon Sauce

*Egg-lemon sauce is a staple in Greek cuisine. It is a light concoction resembling hollandaise sauce, but without the butter. The sauce is delightful on green beans or broccoli and makes the base for the classic **avgolemono** soup.*

1 pound asparagus
2 large eggs
¼ teaspoon dry mustard
Dash hot pepper sauce
4 or 5 tablespoons lemon juice
1 teaspoon cornstarch
6 tablespoons chicken stock
⅛ teaspoon freshly ground pepper

Break off and discard tough ends of asparagus. Boil, covered, in 2 inches salted water for 4 to 7 minutes, or until crisp-tender. Drain and keep warm.

In a double boiler, mix eggs, mustard, hot pepper sauce and lemon juice. Combine cornstarch with stock. Add to egg mixture; season lightly with pepper and blend with a whisk. Cook over hot water, stirring constantly, for 6 to 8 minutes, or until thickened. Remove from heat. Place asparagus in a serving dish, pour the sauce over it, and serve at once.

Galaktoboureko
Custard Pastry

Syrup:
1½ cups sugar
1 cup water
2 teaspoons grated orange peel
1 cinnamon stick

Custard:
1 quart milk
¼ cup butter
½ cup sugar
½ cup farina (cream of wheat)
5 eggs
½ cup orange juice
1 teaspoon vanilla

Pastry:
10 sheets *filo* dough
½ cup unsalted butter, melted

Gently boil sugar, water, orange peel and cinnamon for 5 minutes. Let cool while preparing custard.

In a large saucepan, scald milk and butter. Add sugar and heat, stirring until dissolved. Gradually pour in farina, stirring constantly. Slowly bring the mixture to a boil; remove from heat. In a large bowl, beat eggs until light; stir in farina mixture, orange juice and vanilla. Let custard cool.

Butter a 7½ × 11½ × 2-inch baking dish and line with one sheet of *filo*, letting dough overlap sides of dish. Keep remaining *filo* covered with plastic wrap and a damp cloth. Brush with melted butter and repeat with four more sheets of *filo*. Pour in cool custard, cover with one sheet of *filo*, cut or folded to fit top of dish, and brush with butter. Layer four more buttered *filo* sheets on top, cutting or folding in the layers that overlap the sides of the pan. With a razor blade or sharp knife, score the top layers into squares or diamonds.

Bake at 400°F for 10 minutes; reduce heat to 350°F and continue baking 45 minutes longer, or until custard is set. Remove pan to a rack and let cool 5 minutes. Slowly pour cool syrup over pastry. Cut into squares or diamonds, following razor lines. Serve warm or cold.

Makes 16 pieces.

*Greek coffee (**kafes**) is prepared in the same manner as Turkish coffee, described on page 171.*

When the guests arrive at an Indian dinner, the entire meal is already on the table. Typically, a meat or fish dish is served only once every two or three days, but there is always a **dal** (legume), several vegetables, bread or rice, and a chutney. A sweet is included here for Western tastes.

INDIA

Tandoori Murgh
Tandoori Chicken

Musur Dal
Lentils and Spinach

Kheera ka Rayta
Cucumbers and Tomatoes with Yogurt

Baingun Bharta
Eggplant and Tomatoes

Matar Soya Pullau
Rice with Green Peas and Fresh Dill

Papitay aur Khajur ki Meethi Chatni
Papaya and Date Chutney

Nan
Flat Soda Bread

Phal ka Salaad
Fruit Salad with Thickened Milk

Tandoori Murgh
Tandoori Chicken

Garam masala, a mixture of spices, is used in many Indian recipes. It may be purchased ready-mixed, or blended to taste as in the recipe below.

4 cups yogurt, divided
3 tablespoons lemon juice
3 cloves garlic, minced
2 tablespoons paprika
1 tablespoon *garam masala**
1½ teaspoons coriander seeds
1 teaspoon cumin
1 teaspoon salt
1 teaspoon cayenne
1-inch piece ginger root, grated
3 chickens, disjointed and skinned, or 6 whole breasts

* *Garam Masala: In a coffee grinder or food processor, grind together ¼ cup black peppercorns, ¼ cup coriander seeds, 3 tablespoons caraway seeds, 1 tablespoon cloves and 20 large cardamoms (coats removed). Add 1 tablespoon cinnamon. Store in an airtight container.*

Mix 2 cups yogurt with all other ingredients except chicken. Coat chicken pieces with mixture. Marinate 24 hours in refrigerator.

Roast on a rack in an oven pan at 400°F. Turn pieces after 30 minutes. Test for doneness after 45 minutes.

When chicken is done, strain juices, whisk in remaining yogurt and heat until barely hot. Serve as sauce for chicken and a dip for *Nan* (see page 78).

Chicken roasted in a hooded grill over hot charcoal approximates the traditional **tandoori** *oven method.*

Masur Dal
Red Lentils and Spinach

¾ cup dried lentils
1½ cups water
½ pound fresh spinach, chopped
2 teaspoons vegetable oil
3 tablespoons chopped onion
Pinch of turmeric
½ teaspoon salt
¼ teaspoon cayenne

Put lentils and water in a 2½-quart saucepan. Bring to a boil, reduce heat, add spinach and simmer 20 minutes, or until lentils are tender.

Saute onion in oil until lightly browned. Stir in turmeric, salt and cayenne. Add to lentils. Serve in small bowls.

Kheera ka Rayta
Cucumbers and Tomatoes with Yogurt

2 teaspoons cumin
2 medium cucumbers
2 tablespoons finely chopped onion
1 tablespoon salt
2 cups yogurt
2 small firm, ripe tomatoes, cut in ½-inch cubes
2 tablespoons finely chopped fresh coriander

Toast cumin in an ungreased skillet over low heat for 30 seconds.

Peel cucumber and halve lengthwise. Scoop out seeds and slice thinly. Combine cucumber, onion and salt in a bowl and let sit at room temperature for 5 minutes. Drain and squeeze gently to remove excess liquid. Add yogurt, tomato, coriander and cumin. Toss gently to coat. Cover tightly and refrigerate at least 1 hour before serving.

Baingun Bharta
Eggplant and Tomatoes

2 medium eggplants (about 2 pounds)
3 tablespoons vegetable oil
1 medium onion, minced
⅓ cup sliced green onion
2 small green hot peppers, minced
¾ teaspoon turmeric
1½ cups peeled, chopped tomato
¼ teaspoon black pepper
1 tablespoon lemon juice
½ teaspoon *garam masala* (see page 74)
1 tablespoon chopped fresh coriander

    Wrap eggplants tightly in aluminum foil and bake at 350°F for 1 hour and 40 minutes. Turn oven off and leave inside 10 to 15 minutes longer.

    Stir-fry onion, green onion, hot peppers and turmeric in oil for 3 minutes. Add tomato and black pepper; cook 5 minutes.

    Peel eggplants. Mash and add to tomato mixture. Cook over low heat, stirring occasionally, for 5 to 10 minutes, or until half the liquid has evaporated. Stir in lemon juice, *garam masala* and coriander.

Matar Soya Pullau
Rice with Green Peas and Fresh Dill

2 tablespoons vegetable oil
⅔ cup finely diced onion
1 tablespoon grated ginger root
½ tablespoon *garam masala* (see page 74)
1 teaspoon crushed cumin seed
2 cups long-grain brown rice
3 cups peas
3½ cups water
½ cup coarsely chopped fresh dill leaves

In a heavy 5-quart pot, saute onion in oil until golden-brown. Add ginger and saute 2 minutes, or until light brown. Stir in *garam masala* and cumin; cook 30 seconds.

Add rice and saute 4 to 5 minutes. Add peas and cook, stirring, another 2 to 3 minutes. Stir in water. Bring to a boil; reduce heat to low, cover tightly and simmer 40 minutes, or until water is completely absorbed. Gently stir in dill leaves, reserving a few to sprinkle on top as garnish.

Papitay aur Khajur ki Meethi Chatni
Papaya and Date Chutney

2 tablespoons vegetable oil
½ tablespoon grated ginger root
2 semi-ripe papayas, peeled, seeded and finely chopped
1 cup chopped dates
1 teaspoon ground coriander seeds
⅛ teaspoon cinnamon
½ teaspoon chili powder
½ tablespoon unsulfured molasses
½ tablespoon honey
¼ cup white vinegar, divided
¼ cup lemon juice
1 teaspoon *garam masala* (see page 74)

In a large skillet with a cover, saute ginger in oil until lightly browned. Add papaya, dates, coriander, cinnamon and chili powder; fry 2 minutes over moderate heat. Stir in molasses, honey and 2 tablespoons vinegar; cook, stirring, for 5 minutes. Reduce heat to low and simmer, covered, for 10 minutes.

Add remaining vinegar, lemon juice and *garam masala*. Simmer, covered, for 30 minutes, occasionally stirring and mashing. Chutney is ready when most of the papaya and dates are mashed and pulpy.

Makes about 1 cup.

Nan
Flat Soda Bread

4 cups flour
1 tablespoon sugar
1 tablespoon baking powder
¼ teaspoon baking soda
1/2 teaspoon salt
2 eggs, lightly beaten
½ cup milk
½ cup yogurt
2 tablespoons oil

In a deep bowl, mix flour, sugar, baking powder, baking soda and salt. Make a well and add eggs, milk, yogurt and oil. Mix until dough is sticky. Knead 5 minutes. Put into a greased bowl. Cover with a damp towel and let rest 3 hours in a warm place.

Coat hands with oil and divide dough into eight parts. Pat each to a ⅜-inch thickness in a teardrop shape. Arrange on a hot, ungreased baking sheet and bake at 450°F for 10 minutes, or until lightly browned. Serve warm.

Makes 8.

*Each **nan** is formed into a teardrop shape, to resemble the traditional shape achieved when the dough is stuck to the side of the kiln-like tandoori oven for baking.*

Phal ka Salaad
Fruit Salad with Thickened Milk

15-ounce can evaporated milk
2 tablespoons unsulfured molasses
2 tablespoons honey
3 ripe mangoes or peaches, peeled and cubed
1 apple, diced
1 banana, sliced
1 orange, peeled and sliced
2 tablespoons unsalted pistachio nuts

Bring milk to a boil. Reduce heat to medium-high and whisk continuously until reduced to 1 cup. Scrape cream from the sides and stir back into milk. Add molasses and honey; whisk until dissolved. Let cool.

Gently stir all the fruit into the milk. Pour into a serving bowl and garnish with nuts. Refrigerate and serve chilled.

A rice table offers small tastes of many dishes. For a family dinner, a small rice table must contain at least seven dishes, but for a major occasion, there may be 30 or 40 dishes, with various side dishes, sauces and chutneys combining to offer an almost infinite variety of flavors, textures, colors and aromas. This is a good dinner for multiple cooks. Begin the meal with a platter of fresh fruit — bananas, pineapple, lychees, mango, kiwis — whatever is in season.

INDONESIAN
RIJSTTAFEL
Rice Table

Bahmi Goreng
Sauteed Noodles

Nasi Kuning
Yellow Rice

Lumpia
Egg Rolls

Saté Babi
Skewered Pork

Gado Gado
Vegetables in Peanut Sauce

Sambal Buncis
Green Beans in Spicy Sauce

Rempeyek
Peanut Fritters

Buah Rujak
Hot-Sweet Salad

Ayam Opor
Chicken in Coconut Milk

Rempah Kelapa
Fried Coconut Balls

Pisang Goreng
Sauteed Bananas

Kecap Manis
Indonesian Soy Sauce

*This is an essential ingredient in Indonesian cuisine and is used in many of the following recipes. **Kecap** is pronounced "ketchup."*

1 cup firmly packed dark brown sugar
1 cup water
1 cup soy sauce
6 tablespoons dark molasses
1 teaspoon grated fresh ginger
½ teaspoon ground coriander seeds
½ teaspoon freshly ground pepper

Combine sugar and water in a 2-quart saucepan. Simmer, stirring, until sugar dissolves. Boil rapidly for 5 minutes, or until syrup reaches 200°F on a candy thermometer. Reduce heat to low, stir in remaining ingredients and simmer 3 minutes.

Makes about 3 cups.

***Kecap manis** will keep two to three months tightly covered and refrigerated.*

Bahmi Goreng
Sauteed Noodles

1½ pounds lean pork, cut into thin strips
¾ cup beef broth
1½ teaspoons salt, divided
4 tablespoons oil
5 cloves garlic, finely minced
1½ teaspoons grated ginger root
1½ tablespoons lemon juice
¼ teaspoon pepper
3 cups shredded cabbage
¾ pound bean sprouts
1½ cups bamboo shoots, cut into thin strips
3 leeks, white part only, chopped
¾ pound Chinese snow pea pods, cut in half diagonally
5 tablespoons *kecap manis* (see page 82)
1½ pounds Indonesian or Chinese noodles

Simmer pork in beef broth, seasoned with ½ teaspoon salt, for 10 minutes; drain and set aside. (Broth may be reserved for other uses.)

Saute garlic and ginger in oil for 2 minutes. Add lemon juice, 1 teaspoon salt and pepper. Add pork, cabbage, sprouts, bamboo shoots, leeks and pea pods; saute 5 minutes longer. Stir in *kecap manis*. Taste for seasoning.

Boil noodles in salted water until cooked but firm; drain. Combine with pork and vegetables.

Nasi Kuning
Yellow Rice

3 cups coconut milk
1½ cups long-grain rice
½ teaspoon salt
1 bay leaf
½ teaspoon turmeric
¼ teaspoon ground coriander seeds
¼ teaspoon pepper
1 egg, beaten
½ cucumber, sliced
½ cup Spanish peanuts
½ cup canned fried onion flakes

Bring coconut milk to a boil; stir in rice, salt, bay leaf, turmeric, coriander and pepper. Reduce heat to low, cover and simmer 20 minutes, or until rice is tender and liquid is absorbed.

Pour egg into a nonstick skillet and cook over low heat, without stirring, until set. Roll up and cut into thin strips.

Garnish rice with egg strips, cucumber, peanuts and onion flakes.

Lumpia
Egg Rolls

2 tablespoons peanut oil
2 tablespoons diced onion
1 clove garlic, minced
¼ pound lean pork, cut into thin strips
¼ pound shelled shrimp, coarsely chopped
½ cup green beans, cut diagonally in ¼-inch lengths
1 small sweet potato, peeled and grated
1 cup shredded cabbage
1 cup bean sprouts, washed and drained
2 tablespoons *kecap manis* (see page 82)
12 egg roll wrappers
1 cup peanut oil

Saute onion and garlic in oil over high heat for 1 minute. Add pork and saute until pink color disappears. Add shrimp and saute until barely pink. Reduce heat to medium-low. Add green beans, sweet potato, cabbage, bean sprouts and *kecap manis;* mix thoroughly. Cover and cook 3 minutes, or until vegetables are crisp-tender.

Spread 2 tablespoons of mixture lengthwise on each egg roll wrapper. Fold over flap along length of filling, then fold up 2 flaps at ends of filling; moisten edge of last flap with water and fold to seal.

Deep-fry in 350°F oil, seam-side down, for 5 minutes, or until golden-brown. Drain on paper towels and keep warm.

Serve with *kecap manis*.

Saté Babi
Skewered Pork

1½ cups coconut milk
3 tablespoons finely chopped onion
5 teaspoons lemon juice, divided
1 tablespoon peanut butter
1 tablespoon turmeric
1 tablespoon brown sugar
2 teaspoons ground coriander seeds
1½ teaspoons cumin
1½ teaspoons salt
1 teaspoon ground chili paste (*sambal ulek*)
½ teaspoon shrimp paste (*trassi*), optional
¼ teaspoon cardamom
2 garlic cloves, minced
1½ pounds boneless pork, cut in ¾-inch cubes
4 tablespoons peanut oil
½ cup *kecap manis* (see page 82)

For marinade, combine coconut milk, onion, 2 teaspoons lemon juice, peanut butter, turmeric, sugar, coriander, cumin, salt, chili paste, shrimp paste, cardamom and garlic. Stir pork into marinade and store, covered, in refrigerator overnight.

Drain pork, reserving marinade. Thread cubes on 6-inch bamboo skewers, using 5 cubes per skewer. Heat oil and place skewers in a skillet and cook, turning and basting with reserved marinade, until brown on all sides.

Simmer remaining marinade with *kecap manis* and remaining lemon juice for 5 minutes and serve as a dipping sauce.

Gado Gado
Vegetables in Peanut Sauce

1 cup shredded cabbage
1 cup sliced carrots
1 cup green beans, cut in 1-inch pieces
1 small cauliflower, separated into florets
1 cup snow peas
1 quart water, with 1 teaspoon salt
1 cup bean sprouts
2 hard-cooked eggs, sliced
1 medium cucumber, sliced
½ cup canned fried onion flakes
1 cup shrimp crackers (*krupuk*)
½ cup chunky peanut butter
1 clove garlic, minced
1 tablespoon brown sugar
1 tablespoon lemon juice
Salt and pepper to taste

Blanch cabbage, carrots, beans, cauliflower and pea pods separately, but in the same lightly salted water, for 3 minutes each. Reserve water. Arrange vegetables in an attractive pattern on a platter. Place bean sprouts on top. Arrange egg slices, cucumber slices, onion flakes and shrimp crackers around vegetables.

In a 1½-quart saucepan, combine peanut butter, garlic, sugar, lemon juice and 1 cup of the vegetable water; simmer 2 minutes. Season with salt and pepper. If sauce is too thick, add more vegetable water.

Pass bowl of sauce to spoon over each serving.

Sambal Buncis
Green Beans in Spicy Sauce

½ small onion
1 clove garlic
1 tablespoon ground chili paste (*sambal ulek*)
1 teaspoon shrimp paste (*trassi*)
½ teaspoon sugar
½ teaspoon salt
2 tablespoons peanut oil
2 tablespoons water
1 tablespoon lemon juice
2 cups green beans, cut in 1-inch pieces
¾ cup coconut milk

In a food processor, grind to a paste the onion, garlic, chili paste, shrimp paste, sugar and salt. Saute in oil for 2 minutes. Add water, lemon juice and beans. Saute another 2 minutes. Add coconut milk and simmer, stirring, until almost dry.

Rempeyek
Peanut Fritters

1 cup Spanish peanuts
2 cups coconut milk
¾ cup flour
2 cloves garlic, minced
1 tablespoon ground coriander seeds
2 teaspoons turmeric
1 teaspoon ginger
½ teaspoon ground chili paste (*sambal ulek*)
½ teaspoon salt
¼ teaspoon cumin
½ cup peanut oil

Soak peanuts in warm water for 1 hour; drain. Stir together coconut milk, flour, garlic, coriander, turmeric, ginger, chili paste, salt and cumin. Add peanuts.

In very hot oil, drop in 2 tablespoons batter for each fritter. Fry until crisp and brown on both sides, turning once. Drain on paper towels.

Buah Rujak
Hot-Sweet Salad

3 tablespoons brown sugar
1 tablespoon ground chili paste (*sambal ulek*)
1 tablespoon lemon juice
1 teaspoon salt
2 tablespoons peanut oil
½ cup coconut milk
2 tablespoons *kecap manis* (see page 82)
2 oranges, peeled and sectioned
1 grapefruit, peeled and sectioned
2 firm pears, cut in 1-inch chunks
¼ melon, cut in 1-inch chunks
2 green apples, cut in 1-inch chunks
1 cup pineapple chunks
1 cucumber, peeled, seeded and cut in 1-inch chunks
4 tablespoons ginger in syrup, drained and chopped

Make a paste of brown sugar, chili paste, lemon juice and salt. Saute in oil for 2 minutes. Add coconut milk and *kecap manis*; let cool.

Combine oranges, grapefruit, pears, melon, apples, pineapple, cucumber and ginger. Mix cooled sauce with fruit. Refrigerate at least 2 hours before serving.

Ayam Opor
Chicken in Coconut Milk

2 chickens, skinned and cut in small pieces
3 tablespoons peanut oil
2 cloves garlic
1 large onion, quartered
½-inch piece fresh ginger root, peeled
1 tablespoon coriander seeds
2 teaspoons cumin
1 teaspoon ground chili paste (*sambal ulek*)
¼ teaspoon cloves
¼ teaspoon cinnamon
3 bay leaves
2 tablespoons mild honey
2 teaspoons lemon juice
1 teaspoon *kecap manis* (see page 82)
½ teaspoon salt
2 cups coconut milk

Fry chicken in oil over medium-high heat for 5 to 10 minutes, or until golden-brown. Remove to paper towels. Reserve oil.

Chop garlic for 5 seconds in a food processor or blender. Add onion and ginger; process another 5 seconds. Add coriander, cumin, chili paste, cloves, cinnamon and bay leaves. Process 10 seconds to a paste.

Add paste to oil in which chicken was cooked. Saute 3 to 5 minutes, or until paste is brown. Add honey, lemon juice, *kecap manis* and salt. Saute 2 minutes. Slowly stir in coconut milk. Bring to a boil; add chicken. Reduce heat, cover and simmer 30 to 40 minutes, or until chicken is tender.

Rempah Kelapa
Fried Coconut Balls

¼ cup chopped onion
4 cloves garlic, minced
2 tablespoons ground coriander seeds
1 teaspoon salt
1 teaspoon ginger
2 cups grated unsweetened coconut
¼ cup flour
2 eggs, lightly beaten
½ teaspoon pepper
¾ cup peanut oil
1 cup *kecap manis* (see page 82)
2 tablespoons lime juice

Grind onion, garlic, coriander, salt and ginger into a paste. Combine with coconut, flour, egg and pepper. Shape into 1-inch balls and fry in hot oil until golden-brown on all sides. Remove to paper towels. Serve with *kecap manis* mixed with lime juice.

Pisang Goreng
Sauteed Bananas

5 firm ripe bananas, peeled
¼ cup lime juice
¼ teaspoon nutmeg
¼ cup peanut oil
2 tablespoons honey

Cut bananas in half lengthwise; dip in lime juice. Sprinkle both sides with nutmeg. Over medium-high heat, saute bananas in oil for 3 to 5 minutes, turning to brown both sides. Reduce heat; drizzle honey over bananas and cook 5 minutes. Serve hot.

Italian food is more than pasta and pizza. The Italians are ingenious cooks, making the most of what is available. In the cooler north, dishes are often based on dairy products, whereas in the hotter southern areas, olive oil and tomato sauce are the staples.

ITALY

Antipasto Misto
Mixed Appetizers

Gnocchi alla Romana
Cheese-Topped Semolina Cakes

Bracchiole
Stuffed Beef Roll

Riso con Funghi
Rice with Mushrooms

Broccoli con Pignoli
Broccoli with Pine Nuts

Focaccia al Rosmarino
Rosemary Flat Bread

Insalata Mista
Mixed Salad with Basil Dressing

Torta di Ricotta
Ricotta Cheese Cake

Caffè
Coffee

Antipasto Misto
Mixed Appetizers

Antipasto is a cold platter composed of virtually any combination of meat, cheese and vegetable (marinated or fresh), attractively arranged on a platter with olives.

The following provide ideas for more variety:
> Canned tuna in olive oil
> Sardines
> Celery stuffed with Gorgonzola cheese
> Pickled mushrooms
> Sliced fennel
> Artichoke hearts

Gnocchi alla Romana
Cheese-Topped Semolina Cakes

3 cups milk
½ teaspoon salt
Pinch of nutmeg
Freshly ground pepper
¾ cup semolina or farina
2 eggs, lightly beaten
1 cup freshly grated Romano cheese, divided
¼ cup melted butter

In a 2- to 3-quart saucepan, bring milk, salt, nutmeg and a few grindings of pepper to a boil over medium heat. Gradually add semolina so the milk never stops boiling, stirring constantly. Continue cooking and stirring until mixture is so thick the spoon will stand unsupported in the middle of the pan. Remove from heat.

Add egg and ¾ cup cheese to semolina and blend well. Spoon onto a buttered baking sheet and spread ¼ inch thick, using a metal spatula dipped in hot water. Refrigerate at least 1 hour, or until firm.

Cut dough into circles or triangles. Transfer to a buttered baking dish. Drizzle with butter and sprinkle remaining cheese on top. (Recipe can be made ahead to this point. Cover with plastic wrap and refrigerate until ready to bake.)

Bake at 400°F for 15 minutes, or until crisp and golden. Put under a hot broiler for 30 seconds to brown. Serve hot.

Bracchiole
Stuffed Beef Roll

3 pounds very lean ground beef
1½ cups fresh fine bread crumbs
1 cup water
2 eggs
3 tablespoons chopped parsley
2 cloves garlic, minced
½ teaspoon pepper
¾ pound ground ham or smoked turkey
⅓ cup grated Parmesan or Romano cheese
¼ cup chopped raisins
¼ cup pine nuts
Olive oil

Sauce:
6 ounces tomato paste
2 cups red wine
1 teaspoon dried basil

Mix beef, bread crumbs, ¾ cup water, eggs, parsley, garlic and pepper. Place mixture on foil; pat out into a rectangle about 8 × 12 inches and ½ inch thick. Cover with a layer of ham or turkey. Sprinkle with cheese, raisins and pine nuts. Roll up like a jelly roll. Cover and chill to firm.

Brown whole surface in oil. Place in a 9 × 13-inch baking dish. Mix tomato paste, wine, ¼ cup water and basil. Spread on meat. Cover dish and bake at 350°F for 1½ hours. Remove from oven and let rest 10 minutes; slice.

Riso con Funghi
Rice with Mushrooms

The mushrooms in this dish resemble wild rice.

¾ cup butter, divided
2 cups long-grain white rice
4 cups boiling water
½ cup chopped onion
1 pound raw mushrooms, finely grated in processor
¼ cup chopped parsley
1 teaspoon salt
½ teaspoon pepper

In a 3-quart flameproof casserole, saute rice in ½ cup butter for 2 to 3 minutes. Pour boiling water over rice; cover and simmer 20 minutes.

Saute onion in remaining butter until soft. Mix into hot, cooked rice. Add mushrooms, parsley, salt and pepper. Mix well. Bake uncovered at 350°F for 20 minutes.

This dish holds well if dinner is delayed.

Broccoli con Pignoli
Broccoli with Pine Nuts

3 pounds broccoli, stems peeled, cut into long stalks
3 tablespoons olive oil
3 tablespoons pine nuts
4 teaspoons fresh lemon juice
Salt and freshly ground pepper to taste

Steam broccoli until crisp-tender, 8 to 10 minutes depending on thickness of stalks. Rinse under cold water to stop cooking. (Broccoli can be cooked up to 1 day ahead and refrigerated.)

Saute nuts in olive oil over medium heat for 3 minutes. Increase heat to medium-high; add broccoli and cook until stalks are heated through, turning occasionally. Transfer to a serving platter. Sprinkle with lemon juice; season with salt and pepper. Serve immediately.

Focaccia al Rosmarino
Rosemary Flat Bread

2 packages dry yeast
1 teaspoon sugar
1½ cups warm water (120° to 130°F)
3 to 4 cups flour
1 teaspoon salt
1 tablespoon olive oil

Topping:
2 to 3 tablespoons olive oil
Salt and pepper to taste
½ teaspoon rosemary

Dissolve yeast and sugar in water. Combine 3 cups flour and salt in a large bowl; stir in yeast mixture and oil. Add enough of the remaining flour to make a stiff dough. Knead 6 minutes, or until smooth and elastic. Let rise 1 hour, or until double. Punch down and flatten into a circle 1 inch thick on a lightly greased pizza pan. Let rise 30 minutes. Make indentations ¼ inch deep with finger tips and drizzle with olive oil; sprinkle with salt, pepper and rosemary. Bake at 400°F for 25 to 30 minutes, or until lightly browned. Cut into wedges and serve.

Insalata Mista
Mixed Salad with Basil Dressing

6 tablespoons extra virgin olive oil
3 tablespoons red wine vinegar
½ cup lightly packed fresh basil leaves, finely chopped
¼ cup chopped green onion
3 tablespoons grated Parmesan cheese
½ teaspoon dry mustard
¼ teaspoon pepper
1 small cucumber
2 small tomatoes
3 quarts lightly packed bite-size pieces mixed salad greens
8-ounce can garbanzo beans, drained
½ cup croutons

Combine oil, vinegar, basil, onion, cheese, mustard and pepper; set aside. (Basil will darken if prepared more than 2 hours ahead.) Peel cucumber and slice very thinly. Cut tomatoes into thin wedges.

In a large bowl, layer greens, cucumber and garbanzos. Arrange tomatoes on top. (Salad may be refrigerated up to 2 hours at this point.) Mix dressing well, toss lightly with salad, sprinkle with croutons and serve.

Torta di Ricotta
Ricotta Cheese Cake

Filling:
4 whole eggs
4 egg yolks
1 pound ricotta cheese
⅓ cup sugar
½ cup almonds, blanched and ground
2 or 3 bitter almonds, ground, optional
½ teaspoon freshly grated lemon peel

Crust:
2 cups flour
½ cup sugar
½ cup cold butter
1 whole egg and 1 egg yolk, beaten

For filling, beat eggs well. Add ricotta, sugar, ground almonds and lemon peel, and beat well.

For crust, mix together flour and sugar. Cut in butter. Mix in eggs. Refrigerate at least 1 hour. Roll out dough and lay in a 9-inch quiche pan with a removable bottom, or a 9-inch pie plate; trim. Pour ricotta mixture into crust. Cut ½-inch strips with remaining dough and make a lattice top. Bake at 350°F for 1 hour. Serve chilled.

The presentation of a Japanese dinner is very important. The color and the form of foods are as carefully considered as taste. With this menu, there will be nine small dishes of food at each person's place, each arranged and garnished with care.

JAPAN

Beer   *Sake* on Ice

Sushi
Vinegared Rice Appetizers

Horenso no Ohitashi
Spinach with Sesame Seeds

Misoyaki
Salmon with Soybean Paste

Nasu
Marinated Eggplant

Gohan
Rice

Suimono
Clear Soup

Tori no Teriyaki
Chicken *Teriyaki*

Sunomono
Squid or Clams in Sweet-Sour Dressing

Kyuri no Sunomono
Cucumber Salad

Takuwan
Pickled Japanese White Radish

Warm *Sake*

Yokan
Jellied Red Bean Paste

Ocha
Green Tea

Sushi
Vinegared Rice Appetizers

Sushi Rice
¼ cup rice vinegar
¼ cup sugar
1½ teaspoons salt
1½ tablespoons *sake*
6 cups cooked rice (make 1 recipe for *Gohan*, page 105)

Combine vinegar, sugar, salt and *sake*. Bring to a boil. Let cool to room temperature. Pour over partially cooled rice and mix thoroughly. (Rice may be covered and left at room temperature for as long as 5 hours before using.)

Nori Maki Sushi
Vegetable *Sushi*

Mushroom *Sushi*
5 dried *shiitake* mushrooms
2 cups cold water
2 tablespoons sugar
2 tablespoons Japanese soy sauce*
2 sheets *nori* seaweed
2 cups *sushi* rice (recipe above)

Soak mushrooms in cold water for 30 minutes. Reserve water. Cut off and discard stems; slice mushrooms into ¼-inch wide strips. Mix with 1 cup reserved water, sugar and soy sauce. Bring to a boil over high heat. Remove mushrooms and continue to boil until liquid is reduced to ¼ cup. Replace mushrooms in liquid and let cool to room temperature.

Prepare *nori* by passing over a flame or hot burner on one side only, to intensify the color and flavor. Place one sheet, shiny side down, on a bamboo mat or heavy cloth napkin. Spread 1 cup *sushi* rice over most of the *nori* sheet, leaving 2 inches on a short edge. Lay half the mushrooms in a row across the middle of the rice. Using the mat as an aid, roll up *nori*, ending with the side which is exposed. Let rest 5 minutes. Unroll mat and cut *sushi* roll into five or six 1-inch rounds. Repeat with second *nori* and remaining mushrooms.

Makes 10 to 12 rounds.

Pickled Japanese White Radish *Sushi*

1 pickled radish (see recipe for *Takuwan* on page 108),
cut into ¼-inch wide strips

Make 2 rolls (10 to 12 *sushi*) in the same manner as for mushroom *sushi*.

Nigiri Sushi
Raw Fish *Sushi*

1 pound very fresh raw fish (tuna, porgy, sea bass, striped bass or red snapper), sliced across the grain into twenty ¼-inch thick pieces
2 cups *sushi* rice (see page 102)
Green Horseradish Paste *(Wasabi)*: 3 tablespoons horseradish powder mixed with 3 tablespoons cold water

Moisten hands to prevent rice from sticking. Shape 1 tablespoon *sushi* rice into an oblong. Spread ⅛ teaspoon horseradish paste down the center (the remaining paste is used for garnish); top with fish slice. Fish should completely cover the top of rice mound. Repeat with remaining rice and fish.

Makes 20 *sushi*.

Garnish for *sushi* plate

Shredded pickled ginger
Green horseradish paste

Dipping sauce for *sushi*

½ cup soy sauce mixed with 2 tablespoons *sake*

* *Japanese soy sauce, unlike Chinese soy sauce, is fermented. Because its flavor is unique, Japanese recipes should always use Japanese soy sauce.*

Horenso no Ohitashi
Spinach with Sesame Seeds

2 tablespoons sesame seeds
2 tablespoons soy sauce
½ teaspoon sugar
1½ pounds fresh spinach, stems removed

Toast sesame seeds in a skillet and crush in a mortar. Mix with soy sauce and sugar.

Drop spinach into boiling salted water. Return to a boil and cook 30 seconds. Drain and plunge into cold water to stop cooking and preserve color. Gently press out water and cut in strips. Mix with dressing and serve at room temperature.

Misoyaki
Salmon with Soybean Paste

2 pounds salmon fillets, or white fish such as halibut or black cod
5 tablespoons white soybean paste (white *miso*)
2 tablespoons grated ginger root
2 tablespoons soy sauce
1 tablespoon sugar
2 tablespoons *sake*

Mix soybean paste, ginger, soy sauce, sugar and *sake* to a paste. Lay fish, skin side down, in an oiled pan; coat top well with mixture. Bake at 450°F for 10 to 15 minutes, or until coating has dark brown spots and flesh is opaque. Serve at once.

Nasu
Marinated Eggplant

Make a day in advance. Be sure to pick smooth-skinned eggplants. Cut out any marks on the skin, which indicate a spoilage underneath.

1½ pounds eggplant
½ cup soy sauce
¼ cup rice vinegar
¼ cup *sake*
1 small clove garlic, minced
1 tablespoon sesame oil, optional
1 green onion, finely chopped
1 teaspoon grated ginger root

Partially peel eggplant, remove large seeds and cut into 1-inch cubes; steam until tender. Combine remaining ingredients; mix with eggplant and heat through. Leave at room temperature to marinate at least 1 day.

Gohan
Rice

2 cups short-grain rice
2½ cups cold water

Pour rice into a sieve. Stirring, rinse under cold water until the draining water is clear. Transfer to a 3-quart heavy saucepan. Add water and soak rice for 30 minutes. Bring to a boil, cover pan tightly and simmer 10 minutes, or until all water has been absorbed. Reduce heat to its lowest point and simmer undisturbed for 5 minutes. Fluff gently with chopsticks or a fork to separate the grains. Serve at once in rice bowls.

To reheat leftover rice, place in a colander and set over 1½ inches of boiling water in a large, heavy pot. Cover pot tightly and steam for about 5 minutes.

Suimono
Clear Soup

6 cups chicken broth
1 tablespoon sugar
2 teaspoons light soy sauce
10-ounce cake *tofu* (soybean curd)
1 cup green peas
1 cup slivered carrots
1 tablespoon cornstarch
1 tablespoon water

Heat broth. Add sugar and soy sauce. Cut *tofu* into 10 pieces and add to soup. Simmer 5 minutes; add peas and carrots. Simmer 1 minute longer. Remove *tofu*, peas and carrots. Place a piece of *tofu* and a few pieces of vegetable in each soup bowl. Mix cornstarch with water. Stir into broth and simmer 2 minutes until slightly thickened. Ladle into bowls.

*The garnish is important to lend a touch of beauty to the soup. A thin slice of mushroom or lemon, a shrimp or bits of green onion may be floated in the center of each bowl. Other kinds of stock can be the base of clear soup, such as consomme or the traditional fish stock, **dashi**, which can be purchased in instant bags.*

Tori no Teriyaki
Chicken *Teriyaki*

1½ pounds (6 to 8) chicken thighs, boned
¼ cup soy sauce
2 tablespoons *mirin*, or 2 tablespoons *sake* plus 1 tablespoon sugar
¼ cup sugar or honey
1 clove garlic, minced
1 tablespoon grated ginger root
Parsley sprigs, strips of pickled ginger or radish "flowers" for
    garnish

Pierce chicken several times with a fork to allow marinade to penetrate and to prevent shrinking when cooked. Mix soy sauce, *mirin*, sugar, garlic and ginger. Marinate chicken for 30 minutes. Remove from sauce; spread on a baking sheet.

Bake at 325°F for 50 minutes, or until browned. Remove to serving platter.

Reduce sauce until thick. Pour glaze over meat. Slice chicken diagonally ½ inch thick. Garnish with parsley, pickled ginger or radishes cut into the shape of flowers.

Sunomono
Squid or Clams in Sweet-Sour Dressing

1½ pounds cleaned fresh squid (or 24 steamed clams, juice
    reserved)
1 teaspoon salt
10 to 12 green onions, cut into 1½-inch lengths
¼ cup rice vinegar
½ cup white soybean paste (white *miso*)
3 tablespoons sugar
2 tablespoons *sake*
1½ tablespoons dry mustard, mixed with hot water to make
    a dense paste

Slice squid open, butterfly fashion. Cut crosswise into ⅛-inch wide strips. Drop all at once into rapidly boiling water. When water returns to a boil, drain and cool at once under cold running water. Do not overcook. Set aside. If you are substituting clams, shell and slice into narrow strips.

Cook green onions in boiling salted water for 1 minute. Drain and cool immediately under cold running water; set aside.

Mix vinegar, soybean paste, sugar, *sake* and mustard until smooth. Add onions and squid to the sauce and stir gently until well coated. Serve at room temperature.

Kyuri no Sunomono
Cucumber Salad

4 large cucumbers, peeled
½ cup sugar
½ cup rice vinegar
¼ cup soy sauce, optional

Slice cucumbers paper-thin. Mix sugar, vinegar and soy sauce. Toss gently with cucumber. Refrigerate at least 30 minutes. Stir before serving.

The Japanese say the bitterness in a cucumber can be extracted by cutting ½ inch off each end and briskly rubbing the exposed surfaces until a froth forms. This froth is the bitterness leaving the cucumber. When it is washed off, the cucumber will be fresh and sweet.

Takuwan
Pickled Japanese White Radish (*Daikon*)

1 pound Japanese white radish, peeled and cut in 6-inch lengths
⅔ cup sugar
⅓ cup rice vinegar
⅔ cup water
2 tablespoons salt
1 small hot pepper, fresh or dried, optional

Mix sugar, vinegar, water and salt; boil until sugar dissolves. Pack radish lengths tightly into a wide-mouth jar. Add pepper. Cover with hot liquid and screw lid on tightly; let cool. Refrigerate 1 week, or until radish turns yellow. Use as a side dish, in *sushi* rolls or as a garnish.

Yokan
Jellied Red Bean Paste

1 stick gelatinous agar-agar (*kanten*) or 2 packages
    (2 tablespoons) gelatin
2 cups cold water
2 cups sugar
1½ cup cooked red beans (*azuki*), drained and pureed
½ teaspoon salt

Soften agar-agar or gelatin in water. Heat, stirring, until dissolved. Strain liquid if agar-agar is used. Stir in sugar until dissolved. Stir in beans and salt. Pour into an 8-inch square pan and cool. Cut into 16 squares or cut shapes with cookie cutters.

Persimmon paste, chestnut paste or white bean paste may be substituted for the red beans. Agar-agar is derived from seaweed and imparts a different texture from gelatin.

Ocha
Green Tea

2 tablespoons *sencha* (high quality tea served with dinner)
1 to 2 cups boiling water, depending on taste

Pour boiling water into a separate container and set aside. Warm teapot and cups with additional boiling water. When water has cooled to about 175°F, replace hot water in teapot with tea leaves. Pour in reserved water and let steep 1 minute. Pour through strainer into warmed cups. More water can be added if tea becomes too strong.

*Because there are several kinds of green tea, each requiring different quantities and temperatures of water, and different steeping times, follow instructions on package, if you can read them. Many Americans prefer **genmai cha** (rice tea).*

The highly varied regional cuisines of Mexico result from contacts of the numerous Indian cultures with the Spaniards. The Indians of the New World domesticated corn, chiles, beans, potatoes, tomatoes, pumpkins, avocados, chocolate and vanilla. The Spaniards introduced olive oil, rice, wine and frying, using the drippings from roasting meats.

MEXICO

Cacahuates
Oaxacan Peanuts

Enchiladas de Carne
Beef Enchiladas

Sopa Poblana
Village Soup

Mancha Manteles
Chicken and Pork Stew with Fruit

Ensalada de Pico de Gallo
Jicama Salad

Crema de Aguacate
Avocado Cream

Palitos de Piñon
Pine Nut Sticks

Cacahuates
Oaxacan Peanuts

Roast peanuts at least a day ahead, so they will absorb the flavors of the chiles and garlic.

20 small dried red chiles
4 cloves garlic
2 tablespoons olive oil
2 pounds shelled peanuts
1 teaspoon coarse salt
1 teaspoon chili powder

Saute chiles and garlic in oil for 1 minute. Mix with peanuts and spread on a baking sheet. Bake at 350°F for 5 minutes, or until lightly browned.

Sprinkle with salt and chili powder; mix and cool. Store in a covered container for at least 1 day. Remove garlic cloves and chiles before serving. You don't want to lose a friend!

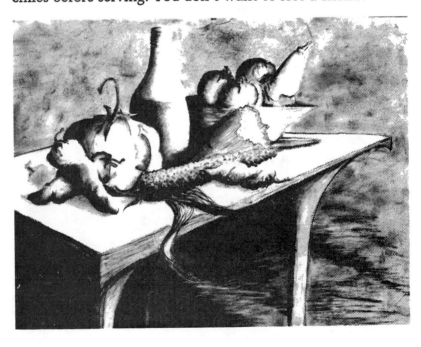

Enchiladas de Carne
Beef Enchiladas

In this menu, the enchiladas are served as appetizers.

2 cups cooked, shredded beef
1½ cups chopped onion
1 clove garlic, minced
⅓ cup vegetable oil
1 tablespoon flour
2 teaspoons chili powder
½ teaspoon salt
¼ teaspoon oregano
¼ teaspoon cumin
¼ teaspoon pepper
15-ounce can tomato sauce
¼ cup water
10 corn tortillas
1 cup shredded Jack or Cheddar cheese
½ cup sour cream
½ cup sliced ripe olives or chopped green onion

Saute beef, onion and garlic in 1 tablespoon oil until onion is lightly browned. Stir in flour, chili powder, salt, oregano, cumin and pepper. Stir in 1½ cups tomato sauce. Simmer, uncovered, for 15 minutes, stirring frequently. Combine remaining tomato sauce and water; heat.

Heat tortillas in a little hot oil until softened. Dip into hot tomato sauce. Spoon ¼ cup meat mixture onto each tortilla and roll up. Place seam side down in a greased baking dish, so they barely touch. Spoon remaining sauce over tortillas and sprinkle with cheese. Bake at 350°F for 20 minutes, or until heated through and cheese is melted.

To serve, spoon sour cream over enchiladas and top with olives or green onions.

Sopa Poblana
Village Soup

The village women will bring to the communal pot whatever produce and meats they have on hand for the occasion. This makes a different soup each time.

1 medium onion, chopped
2 large ripe tomatoes, peeled and chopped
1 tablespoon chopped fresh coriander (*cilantro*)
½ cup vegetable oil
2½ quarts soup stock (chicken, beef, vegetable or fish)
1 package frozen chopped spinach, thawed
Salt and pepper to taste
10 small tortillas, quartered
1 cup shredded white cheese, as crumbly as possible

Saute onion, tomatoes and coriander in 1 tablespoon oil until onion is tender. Add soup stock, spinach, salt and pepper; simmer 30 minutes to blend flavors.

Lightly fry tortilla quarters in remaining hot oil; drop into soup. Ladle into bowls and sprinkle with cheese.

Mancha Manteles
Chicken and Pork Stew with Fruit

Literally, "Tablecloth Stainers."

1 pound boneless pork shoulder, cut in 1-inch cubes
2½ cups water
2 tablespoons peanut oil
2 pounds chicken legs and thighs
1 medium onion, chopped
1 green pepper, chopped
¼ cup almonds
1 tablespoon sesame seeds
8-ounce can tomato sauce
1 tablespoon chili powder
1 teaspoon salt
½ teaspoon cinnamon
2 sweet potatoes, cut in 1-inch pieces
1 cup pineapple chunks
2 apples, peeled and sliced
2 bananas, sliced
2 tablespoons chopped fresh coriander (*cilantro*)

Simmer pork cubes in water to cover for 25 minutes. Skim fat from broth, strain and reserve. Set pork aside.

Saute chicken in hot oil until lightly browned; remove and set aside. In the same skillet, stir-fry pork until lightly browned; remove and set aside. In the same skillet, saute onion, green pepper, almonds and sesame seeds until onion is tender. Discard any remaining fat. Puree with tomato sauce in a food processor or blender until smooth.

Return to skillet the tomato mixture, reserved broth, chili powder, salt and cinnamon; simmer 10 to 15 minutes. Add chicken, pork and sweet potatoes. Simmer, covered, for 45 to 60 minutes. Add water if stew becomes too dry.

Add pineapple and apples. Cover and simmer 10 minutes, or until apples are tender. Stir in bananas and coriander. Serve in soup bowls, accompanied by warm tortillas.

Ensalada de Pico de Gallo
Jicama Salad

Literally, "Rooster's Beak Salad."

3 cups peeled, quartered and thinly sliced jicama
2 oranges, peeled and thinly sliced
1 cucumber, peeled and sliced
1 small mild onion, thinly sliced
1 green bell pepper, thinly sliced
1 head Romaine lettuce, torn
⅓ cup olive oil
3 tablespoons wine vinegar
½ teaspoon oregano
⅛ teaspoon black pepper

In a salad bowl, combine jicama, oranges, cucumber, onion, green pepper and lettuce. Mix oil, vinegar, oregano and black pepper. Toss with salad.

Crema de Aguacate
Avocado Cream

5 avocados
⅓ cup lime juice
1½ cups sugar
2 cups milk

Puree avocados, lime juice and sugar in a blender. Blend in milk. Pour into a container with a lid. Lay plastic wrap on surface to prevent discoloration; cover. Chill several hours.

Palitos de Piñon
Pine Nut Sticks

1 cup butter, room temperature
1¼ cups powdered sugar, divided
2 teaspoons vanilla
2 cups flour
½ teaspoon cinnamon
1 cup pine nuts

Cream butter, ¼ cup powdered sugar and vanilla. Mix in flour, cinnamon and nuts. On a lightly floured board, roll 2-tablespoon portions of dough into sticks ½ inch thick. Cut sticks into 2-inch lengths.

Place sticks 1 inch apart on ungreased baking sheets. Bake at 325°F for 25 minutes, or until light brown.

While cookies are still warm, sift remaining powdered sugar over them. Let cool. Cookies can be stored in an airtight container for 1 week, or frozen for longer periods.

Makes 5 to 6 dozen sticks.

"The food equals the affection." This Middle Eastern proverb requires that an abundant table be set for guests at all times. The responsibility of the guest is to eat enough to show proper regard for the host.

Although each of these recipes comes from a specific culture, most are common throughout the region and cross-culturally, perhaps with slight variations.

MIDDLE EAST

Falafel
Chick Pea Balls

Eggplant-Pine Nut Spread

Israeli Chilled Yogurt-Cucumber Soup

Derevi Sarma
Armenian Stuffed Grape Leaves

Faisinjan
Persian Chicken in Pomegranate Sauce

Rice

Tabbouleh
Lebanese Bulgur Salad

Ma'amoul
Lebanese Pistachio Semolina Cookies

Sarhosh Portakal
Turkish Oranges

Falafel
Chick Pea Balls

2 cups cooked chick peas (garbanzo beans)
1 egg, beaten
2 tablespoons fine bread crumbs
2 tablespoons chopped parsley
1½ tablespoons *tahini* (sesame paste)
2 small cloves garlic, minced
½ teaspoon salt
¼ teaspoon cumin
¼ teaspoon turmeric
⅛ teaspoon cayenne
¼ cup flour
Vegetable oil for frying

Lemon-*Tahini* Dipping Sauce:
½ cup *tahini*
½ cup yogurt
2 tablespoons fresh lemon juice
1 tablespoon minced parsley
1 small clove garlic, minced
¼ teaspoon cumin
⅛ teaspoon salt
Dash cayenne

Mash chick peas well. Combine with egg, bread crumbs, parsley, *tahini*, garlic, salt, cumin, turmeric and cayenne. Chill well.

For dipping sauce, beat together all ingredients until sauce thickens.

With floured hands, form 1-inch balls of chick pea mixture. Lightly dust with flour. Deep-fry in 2 inches hot oil for 5 minutes, or until golden-brown.

Serve immediately with Lemon-*Tahini* Dipping Sauce.

Eggplant-Pine Nut Spread

1 large eggplant, partially peeled
½ cup olive oil
1 large tomato, peeled and chopped
1 clove garlic, minced
2 tablespoons finely chopped onion
½ cup pine nuts
¼ cup finely chopped parsley
1 lemon, cut in wedges
Pita or sesame crackers

Remove stem end from eggplant. Slice eggplant ¼ inch thick. Fry in ¼ cup hot oil until golden-brown on both sides, adding more oil as necessary. Remove to paper towels.

Chop eggplant and put in a bowl. Stir in tomato, garlic, onion and pine nuts. Chill. Sprinkle with parsley and garnish with lemon wedges. Serve with pita or sesame crackers.

Israeli Chilled Yogurt-Cucumber Soup

An ideal dish for hot summer days, this is best when refrigerated at least 10 hours before serving.

1 pound small cucumbers, peeled, seeded and grated
1½ teaspoons chopped fresh dill, or 1/2 teaspoon dried
½ teaspoon olive oil
¼ teaspoon salt
2 cloves garlic, minced
4 cups yogurt

Garnish:
⅓ cup minced walnuts
Mint sprigs

    Season cucumbers with dill, oil, salt and garlic; mix well. Stir in yogurt. If mixture is too thick, add a small quantity of water until desired consistency is reached. Refrigerate.
    Garnish with nuts and mint sprigs before serving.

Derevi Sarma
Armenian Stuffed Grape Leaves

4 cups chopped onions
1 cup white rice, washed
1 cup extra virgin olive oil
¼ cup chopped parsley
¼ cup chopped fresh dill weed, or 1 teaspoon dried
Juice of 1 lemon
¼ cup dried currants
¼ cup pine nuts
1 teaspoon salt
¼ teaspoon pepper
1 jar (50) grape leaves
2 cups cold water
Lemon wedges for garnish

Squeeze chopped onions with hands to soften. Stir in rice, oil, parsley, dill, lemon juice, currants, nuts, salt and pepper.

Rinse grape leaves in warm water; drain. Spread three leaves on the bottom of a large flameproof casserole. Take one of the remaining leaves, cut off stem and place on a small plate, rough side up. Put 1 teaspoon filling near the stem end. Fold over the sides, then roll toward the tip. Place in casserole. Continue rolling and layering the filled leaves in the casserole, each layer lying perpendicular to the layer below. Place a plate inside the casserole and upside down on the rolled leaves. Add water and cover the casserole.

Bring to a boil; lower heat and simmer 1 hour. Remove from heat and let cool completely without uncovering in order to contain the steam. Remove the cover and plate. Holding a large inverted serving plate firmly on the casserole, quickly turn both upside down. Lift casserole off the perfectly formed mound of stuffed grape leaves. Discard the flat leaves from the top.

Garnish with lemon wedges. Serve at room temperature.

Don't refrigerate, or the rice will lose its nice texture. Stuffed grape leaves will keep 2 to 3 days at room temperature.

Faisinjan
Persian Chicken in Pomegranate Sauce

5 tablespoons butter, divided
2 large onions, chopped or sliced
2 large fryer chickens, or 5 whole chicken breasts
14½-ounce can beef bouillon or consomme
1 cup water
2½ cups finely ground walnuts
4 to 5 tablespoons pomegranate syrup
2 to 3 tablespoons sugar
2 tablespoons lemon juice
1 teaspoon salt
½ teaspoon saffron
¼ teaspoon cinnamon
¼ teaspoon nutmeg
¼ teaspoon pepper

Saute onions in 2 tablespoons butter until golden-brown. Remove from pan. Add remaining butter and saute chicken until light brown. Add bouillon and onions. Cover and simmer gently for 30 minutes; cool. Bone chicken and tear into bite-sized pieces.

In a saucepan, gently simmer in water the walnuts, syrup and sugar for 10 to 15 minutes.

Combine chicken, the sauce in which it cooked and the walnut mixture. Add lemon juice, salt, saffron, cinnamon, nutmeg and pepper. Cover and simmer gently for 1 hour. Add a little sugar if too sour, or more pomegranate syrup if too sweet. The chicken should be coated with a generous quantity of rich, dark, sweet-sour sauce. Serve with rice.

This recipe may also be made with meatballs or cubed lamb.

Tabbouleh
Lebanese Bulgur Salad

1¼ cups water
2 teaspoons salt, divided
¾ cup bulgur wheat
3 cups finely chopped parsley
2 cups tomatoes, peeled and chopped
¾ cup finely chopped fresh mint
¾ cup finely chopped green onion
½ cup olive oil
¼ cup lemon juice
½ teaspoon freshly ground black pepper

Bring water and 1 teaspoon salt to a boil; stir in bulgur. Cover and remove from heat. Let stand 30 minutes or until all liquid is absorbed. Fluff with a fork. Combine with parsley, tomatoes, mint, onion, oil, lemon juice, remaining salt and pepper.

Let stand at room temperature at least 2 hours before serving.

Ma'amoul
Lebanese Pistachio Semolina Cookies

These traditional Easter cookies are usually formed in molds. Here, they are simply rolled into balls.

1½ cups semolina
1½ cups flour
¼ teaspoon salt
¼ teaspoon baking powder
½ cup granulated sugar, divided
½ pound butter
5 tablespoons rose- or orange-flower water, divided*
1¼ cups finely chopped pistachios or walnuts
¼ teaspoon cinnamon
Powdered sugar for dusting

Mix semolina, flour, salt, baking powder and ¼ cup sugar. Cut in butter. Rub between fingers to make a fine meal. Sprinkle 3 tablespoons flower water plus just enough water to make dough hold together, mixing with a fork until just combined. Cover and let rest 1 hour.

For filling, mix pistachios, 2 tablespoons flower water, remaining sugar and cinnamon.

Form dough into two dozen 1½-inch balls. Make a deep thumbprint in each ball, put 1 tablespoon filling in center and close dough around it, sealing well.

Place on a baking sheet, leaving 2 inches between each ball. Bake at 325°F for 15 to 20 minutes, or until barely golden. Let cool on a rack. Dust with powdered sugar.

* *Use orange water reserved from Turkish Oranges (see recipe on page 127) if flower waters are unavailable.*

Sarhosh Portakal
Turkish Oranges

8 large oranges (1 per person)
1½ cups cold water
2 cups sugar
2 whole cloves
½ cup Grand Marnier liqueur
½ cup Curaçao liqueur
3 tablespoons brandy

Peel oranges, removing white pith. Set aside. Cut pith away from half the peel, and slice cleaned peel into paper-thin slivers. Place in a saucepan with water. Bring to a boil and simmer 3 to 4 minutes. Drain, reserving liquid. Slice oranges and hold together with toothpicks. Place in a serving dish and arrange peel on top.

Make a syrup by mixing sugar and 2 tablespoons reserved orange water in a saucepan; add cloves and cook to a light caramel color. Remove from heat and stir in 3 tablespoons boiling orange water. Cook until caramel has dissolved, stirring constantly. Remove from heat. Add Grand Marnier, Curaçao and brandy; spoon immediately over oranges. Chill 4 to 6 hours, turning oranges from time to time. Serve with fresh cream.

A PACIFIC NORTHWEST BUFFET

Appetizers

Dropped Olives   Artichoke Bites
Cherry Tomatoes with Smoked Salmon Mousse
Wild Mushroom Canapés

Soups

Strawberry Soup
Crab and Avocado Soup

Salads

Melba's Gold-Plated Pickles
M & M Salad   Snow Pea Salad   Lopez Salad

Main Dishes

Salmon Pie   Oyster Pie
Chicken Breasts with Crab
Baked Stuffed Salmon with Cucumber Sauce
Seafood-Mushroom Medley

Vegetables

Potatoes and Broccoli with Pesto
Asparagus and Morels in Beurre Blanc
Layered Cauliflower

Breads

Cranberry Muffins   Cheese Soda Bread

Desserts
Cheesecake with Huckleberry Sauce
Death by Apple Pie
Chocolate Truffle Cake
Chocolate-Dipped Treats

Beverage
Raspberry Spritzer

This buffet is a showcase of Pacific Northwest abundance. Seafoods, fruits, vegetables, herbs and mushrooms provide something for everyone. Unless otherwise stated, each recipe serves 8 to 10. Choose your favorites for a smaller number of guests, or put together this spectacular buffet for 30.

Dropped Olives

1 cup grated Cheddar cheese
2 tablespoons butter
½ cup flour
⅛ teaspoon cayenne
16-ounce can pitted medium black olives, drained

Cream together cheese and butter. Blend in flour and cayenne. Break off 1-inch pieces of dough and mold around each olive. Bake on a cookie sheet at 400°F for 15 minutes.

Artichoke Bites

2 (6-ounce) jars marinated artichoke hearts
1 medium onion, finely chopped
1 clove garlic, minced
5 eggs, slightly beaten
1 cup shredded sharp Cheddar cheese
1 cup shredded Swiss cheese
1 cup grated Parmesan cheese
½ teaspoon basil
¼ teaspoon oregano
¼ teaspoon Tabasco sauce
⅛ teaspoon Worcestershire sauce
½ cup dry bread crumbs

Drain marinade from artichoke hearts, reserving marinade from one jar. Finely chop artichoke hearts. Cook onions and garlic in reserved marinade until soft. Mix together all ingredients. Pour into a greased 9 × 13-inch baking dish and bake at 350°F for 40 minutes, or until set. Cut into 1½-inch squares. Serve hot or at room temperature.

Cherry Tomatoes
with Smoked Salmon Mousse

4 ounces cream cheese
1½ ounces canned smoked salmon, drained, liquid reserved
½ tablespoon grated onion
½ teaspoon Worcestershire sauce
⅛ teaspoon paprika
30 firm cherry tomatoes
½ tablespoon chopped parsley

Cream together cheese, salmon, onion, Worcestershire and paprika. Add liquid from salmon to thin if necessary. Cut off stem end of each tomato and scoop out pulp. Fill centers with mousse. Sprinkle with parsley.

Wild Mushroom Canapés

2 tablespoons chopped onion
2 tablespoons olive oil
1 pound wild mushrooms, finely chopped (Chanterelles or
    Boletus Edulis are best)
1 tablespoon fresh chopped parsley
Pepper to taste
8 ounces cream cheese, room temperature
⅛ teaspoon garlic salt
⅛ teaspoon Worcestershire sauce

Saute onion in oil until translucent; add mushrooms, parsley and pepper. Cook until liquid has evaporated; let cool.
Beat cheese until soft and fluffy; season with garlic salt, pepper and Worcestershire. Add mushroom mixture. Let flavors blend 2 hours or overnight. Serve on water crackers or Melba rounds.

Strawberry Soup

1 quart fresh ripe strawberries
½ cup unsweetened pineapple juice
1 large ripe peach, peeled and sliced
2 cups defatted chicken broth
½ cup light sour cream
2 tablespoons chopped toasted almonds

Puree half the strawberries with pineapple juice in a blender. Add remaining strawberries and peach; blend for 30 seconds. Add broth and blend 30 seconds longer. Chill. Garnish with a dollop of sour cream and toasted almonds.

Crab and Avocado Soup

1 clove garlic
¼ small onion
2 tablespoons unsalted butter
3 tablespoons flour
1 cup milk
3 cups chicken stock
2 ripe medium avocados, cut in 1-inch pieces
2 teaspoons lime juice
¼ teaspoon Tabasco sauce
½ teaspoon salt
⅛ teaspoon white pepper
1 cup (8 ounces) crabmeat
½ cup cream
1 tablespoon minced chives
Lime wedges

Finely chop garlic and onion; set aside. Melt butter; whisk in flour and cook, stirring, for 1 minute. Don't let mixture brown. Add milk; whisk until smooth and thickened. Add stock and onion mixture; simmer, partially covered, for 10 minutes, stirring occasionally. Cool to room temperature.

Puree avocado, lime juice, Tabasco, salt and pepper until smooth. Whisk avocado mixture into stock. Stir in crabmeat and cream. Refrigerate at least 4 hours. Taste for seasoning. Sprinkle with chives and serve with lime wedges.

Melba's Gold-Plated Pickles

Melba Schmitz tells us this is a long-guarded secret, often requested but never before divulged.

12 large slicing cucumbers, or 8 English cucumbers
5 quarts water, divided
1 cup pickling salt
2 quarts vinegar, divided
6 cups (3 pounds) sugar
1 tablespoon mustard seed
1 tablespoon whole cloves
1 tablespoon whole allspice
2 sticks cinnamon
1-inch piece ginger root
2 cloves garlic

Mix 3 quarts water and salt in a large nonreactive container. Completely submerge cucumbers, weighted down, for 3 days; drain. Soak in fresh water for 3 days, changing water daily.

Cook cucumbers in 2 quarts water with 1½ quarts vinegar until crisp-tender. Remove and cut into ½-inch chunks. Return to vinegar solution and let stand 3 days, totally immersed.

Mix sugar, 2 cups vinegar, mustard seed, cloves, allspice, cinnamon, ginger and garlic. Bring to a boil and pour over cucumbers. Weight down; let stand 3 days. Remove cucumbers and pack into sterile jars. Strain syrup, bring to a boil, pour into jars and seal. Process 15 minutes in a boiling water bath.

M & M Salad

1¼ cups dried black beans, soaked overnight and drained
3 cups boiling water
2 chicken bouillon cubes
1 teaspoon salt
1 clove garlic, whole
1 bay leaf
¾ cup olive oil
¼ cup wine vinegar
Juice of 1 lemon
2 cloves garlic, minced
1 tablespoon cumin
1 teaspoon oregano
1 teaspoon Worcestershire sauce
½ teaspoon freshly ground black pepper
1½ cups chicken stock
1½ cups couscous
1 red bell pepper, diced
1 yellow bell pepper, diced
1 green bell pepper, diced
½ cup finely chopped parsley
3 green onions, sliced

To boiling water, add beans, bouillon, whole garlic and bay leaf. Simmer 2 hours, or until beans are tender. Add more water as needed.

Discard garlic and bay leaf. Rinse and drain beans; toss with marinade of oil, vinegar, lemon juice, minced garlic, cumin, oregano, Worcestershire, 1 teaspoon salt and black pepper.

Bring chicken stock to a boil. Stir in couscous. Cover pan, remove from heat and let stand 5 minutes. Fluff with a fork and stir into beans. Refrigerate.

Reserve a few pieces of each color bell pepper for garnish. Mix remaining peppers, parsley and onion with beans. Taste for seasoning. Garnish with reserved peppers. Serve at room temperature.

This can easily be a main dish salad. It also travels well for picnics and potlucks.

Snow Pea Salad

1 pound fresh snow peas, strings removed
3 cups shredded lettuce
1 pound mushrooms, thinly sliced
1 large red bell pepper, seeded and cut in strips
6 green onions, thinly sliced
¼ cup sesame seeds, toasted

Dressing:
⅓ cup oil
2 tablespoons white wine vinegar
1 tablespoon lemon juice
1 tablespoon sugar
1 clove garlic, finely minced

Blanch peas in boiling water for 1 minute. Drain and rinse under cold water. Dry thoroughly. Cut in half diagonally; mix with lettuce, mushrooms, pepper, onions and sesame seeds.

Mix together all dressing ingredients. Toss with salad.

Lopez Salad

2 pounds spinach, large stems removed
1 quart sliced strawberries

Dressing:
½ cup oil
¼ cup fruit or white wine vinegar
½ cup sugar
2 tablespoons poppy seeds
1½ tablespoons minced onion
¼ teaspoon paprika
¼ teaspoon Worcestershire sauce

Thoroughly mix all dressing ingredients. Toss with spinach and strawberries.

Salmon Pie

1 unbaked 9-inch pie shell
3 eggs, slightly beaten
1 cup half-and-half
1 pound leftover cooked salmon, or canned salmon, drained and
    flaked
2 cups grated Monterey Jack cheese
1 teaspoon dill weed
Dash of salt and pepper
1 cup coarsely chopped arugula or spinach

Prick pie shell and bake at 400°F for 10 minutes.

Combine eggs, half-and-half, salmon, cheese, dill, salt and pepper. Pour half of mixture into crust. Layer arugula leaves and cover with remaining egg mixture. Bake at 325°F for 40 to 45 minutes, or until custard is set.

Oyster Pie

1⅔ cups coarsely crumbled saltine crackers
6 tablespoons butter, divided
2 tablespoons water
1 small onion, finely chopped
3 tablespoons flour
1¼ cups milk
Pinch of salt
3 eggs, beaten
1 pint small oysters, drained

Blend crumbs, ¼ cup soft butter and water. Press firmly against bottom and sides of a 9-inch pie plate. Distribute oysters on crust.

Saute onion in remaining butter until soft. Stir in flour. Add milk and salt, stirring constantly until mixture thickens. Cool slightly. Stir in eggs. Pour into shell. Bake at 325°F for 1 hour, or until filling is set.

Chicken Breasts with Crab

5 whole medium chicken breasts
5 tablespoons butter, divided
¼ cup flour
¾ cup milk
¾ cup chicken broth
⅓ cup dry white wine
¼ cup chopped onion
½ cup sliced mushrooms
½ pound fresh crabmeat, or 7-ounce can, drained and flaked
½ cup coarsely crumbled saltine crackers (10 crackers)
2 tablespoons chopped parsley
¼ teaspoon salt
Dash of pepper
1 cup shredded Swiss cheese
½ teaspoon paprika

Skin, bone and halve chicken breasts. Place boned sides up; working from center to edges, pound lightly to flatten.

Melt 3 tablespoons butter; stir in flour. Add milk, broth and wine. Cook, stirring, until thick and bubbly. Set aside.

Saute onion and mushrooms in 1 tablespoon butter until tender but not brown. Stir in crabmeat, cracker crumbs, parsley, salt and pepper. Stir in 2 tablespoons wine sauce. In a greased 9 × 13 × 2-inch baking dish, place chicken with ¼ cup crab mixture under each piece. Pour remaining sauce over all.

Bake, covered, at 350°F for 40 minutes, or until chicken is tender. Uncover. Sprinkle with cheese and paprika. Bake 2 minutes longer, or until cheese melts. Transfer to a serving platter; spoon juices over chicken.

Baked Stuffed Salmon with Cucumber Sauce

3 cups bread crumbs
¼ to ⅓ cup dry white wine
1 large onion, chopped
½ cup chopped celery
4 tablespoons butter
1 teaspoon fresh thyme, or ¼ teaspoon dried
Salt and pepper to taste
⅓ cup seedless golden raisins
5-pound salmon, head removed and butterflied
¼ cup melted butter
1 tablespoon lemon juice
1 teaspoon minced onion

Moisten bread crumbs with wine. Set aside. Saute onion and celery in butter until tender but not brown. Add thyme, salt and pepper. Pour over softened bread. Mix in raisins.

Put stuffing inside salmon and place in a greased baking dish. Combine melted butter, lemon juice and minced onion; brush on salmon. Bake, uncovered, at 350°F for 50 to 60 minutes, or until opaque and moist. Serve with Cucumber Sauce.

Cucumber Sauce

½ cup seeded and shredded cucumber
½ cup sour cream
¼ cup mayonnaise
1 tablespoon chopped chives
2 teaspoons lemon juice
¼ teaspoon salt
Dash of white pepper

Blend all ingredients. Serve at room temperature.

Seafood-Mushroom Medley

6 tablespoons butter, divided
1 pound mushrooms, sliced
2 small leeks, white part only, in fine julienne strips
2 small carrots, in fine julienne strips
2 ribs celery, in fine julienne strips
4 tablespoons minced shallots
3 pounds sea scallops or prawns, or a combination
2 cups dry white wine
½ teaspoon tarragon
½ teaspoon salt
⅛ teaspoon white pepper
1 cup half-and-half
2 teaspoons lemon juice
1 tablespoon finely minced fresh chives

Saute mushrooms, leeks, carrots, celery and shallots in 4 tablespoons butter for 5 minutes, or until vegetables are just tender but not brown. Set aside.

If scallops are large, cut in half. Saute shellfish in 2 tablespoons butter over medium-high heat for 3 minutes, or until they begin to turn opaque. Add wine, tarragon, salt and pepper. Lower heat so liquid barely simmers; poach 3 to 5 minutes, or until cooked through. Do not overcook.

Remove shellfish. Increase heat and cook until liquid is reduced by half. Reduce heat; slowly add half-and-half, stirring constantly. Continue cooking until sauce has thickened. Stir in lemon juice and taste for seasoning.

Return shellfish and vegetables to pan over low heat and heat through. Sprinkle with chives.

Potatoes and Broccoli with Pesto

3 pounds medium new potatoes
2 pounds broccoli, cut in 2-inch pieces
1 cup pesto

Boil potatoes in salted water for 15 minutes, or until just tender. Drain, reserving 1 tablespoon of liquid to mix with pesto. Steam broccoli in ½ inch water for 5 to 7 minutes, or until crisp-tender. Cut potatoes in half. Arrange with broccoli in a serving dish. Mix reserved liquid with pesto and drizzle sauce over all.

Pesto

1½ cups torn fresh basil
½ cup fruity olive oil
2 cloves garlic, minced
¼ cup pine nuts or walnuts
¼ cup grated fresh Parmesan cheese
2 tablespoons lemon juice
⅛ teaspoon salt
⅛ teaspoon pepper

Puree all ingredients in a food processor or blender.

Asparagus and Morels in *Beurre Blanc*

2 ounces dried morels or other wild mushrooms
1 cup boiling water
3 pounds asparagus, cut in 2-inch lengths
10 tablespoons butter
2 tablespoons dry white wine
1 tablespoon white wine vinegar
Salt and freshly ground black pepper to taste

Place morels in a saucepan; cover with water and soak 1 hour. Remove, pat dry and spread on paper towels. Boil the soaking liquid until reduced to 2 tablespoons; set aside.

Stir-fry asparagus in 2 tablespoons butter for 4 minutes. Add morels and stir-fry another 4 to 5 minutes, or until asparagus is crisp-tender.

Add wine and vinegar to reserved mushroom liquid; boil to reduce to 2 tablespoons. Whisk in remaining 8 tablespoons butter, a tablespoon at a time, over very low heat, until sauce is thick and creamy. Season with salt and pepper; pour over asparagus and morels.

Layered Cauliflower

1 large head cauliflower, cut into florets
1 teaspoon lemon juice
1 teaspoon sugar
1 teaspoon salt
3 tablespoons butter
1 large onion, chopped
1 small bell pepper, seeded and chopped
½ pound fresh mushrooms, sliced
½ teaspoon paprika
¼ teaspoon cayenne
1 cup grated Swiss cheese

Boil cauliflower in water to cover with lemon juice, sugar and salt for 3 minutes, or until crisp-tender. Saute onion, bell pepper and mushrooms in butter until soft.

Place half the cauliflower in a buttered 2-quart casserole. Top with half the sauteed vegetables; sprinkle with half the paprika and cayenne, and half the cheese. Repeat layers. Bake uncovered at 350°F for 30 minutes.

Cranberry Muffins

4 cups flour
⅔ cup sugar
5 teaspoons baking powder
1 teaspoon baking soda
2 cups cranberries
Grated peel of 1 orange
2 cups yogurt
⅔ cup vegetable oil
2 eggs, beaten

Mix flour, sugar, baking powder and baking soda. Stir in cranberries and orange peel. In a separate bowl, mix yogurt, oil and eggs. Quickly stir into flour mixture with a fork. Spoon into greased or paper-lined muffin cups and bake at 400°F for 25 minutes, or until lightly brown.
Makes 24.

Cheese Soda Bread

4 cups whole wheat flour
2 cups white flour
½ cup sugar
1½ teaspoons salt
2½ cups (½ pound) grated sharp Cheddar cheese
2 tablespoons grated onion
1 tablespoon dried dill weed
1 quart buttermilk
4 teaspoons baking soda

Stir together flours, sugar and salt. Stir cheese, onion and dill into flour mixture. In a separate bowl, combine buttermilk and baking soda; stir into flour mixture. Do not beat. Pour into two greased 5 × 9 × 3-inch loaf pans. Put in preheated 375°F oven. Immediately reduce temperature to 350°F and bake for 1 hour. Remove from pans and cool on a rack.

Cheesecake with Huckleberry Sauce

2 cups finely crushed graham crackers
½ cup sugar
½ cup melted butter
1 pound cream cheese; or 1 cup cottage cheese, pureed, and
    8 ounces cream cheese
1 cup sugar
4 eggs
2 cups sour cream

Mix crumbs, sugar and butter and press into a 9- or 10-inch springform pan, bringing crust up the sides to 1 inch from top. Bake at 375°F for 8 minutes. Cool on a rack.

Beat together cream cheese and sugar until smooth. Beat in one egg at a time. Stir in sour cream; pour into crust.

Bake at 350°F for 45 minutes. Turn off oven; open door and let stand in oven for 1 hour. When completely cool, loosen edge of cake with a knife, allowing top ridge of crust to drop around edge of filling. Cover with plastic wrap and refrigerate overnight. Serve with Huckleberry Sauce.

Huckleberry Sauce

3 cups huckleberries or blueberries
¼ cup sugar
3 tablespoons water, divided
1½ tablespoons cornstarch
2 tablespoons orange-flavored liqueur

Mix huckleberries, sugar and 1 tablespoon water in a saucepan. Slowly bring to a boil over low heat. Simmer 5 minutes. Blend cornstarch and remaining water. Slowly stir into berries. Simmer until mixture thickens and is clear. Remove from heat and add liqueur; cool. Spoon over slices of cheesecake.

Death by Apple Pie

This rich and delectable pie won a first prize for one of our members from the Washington State Apple Commission.

Crust:
2 cups sifted flour
1 teaspoon salt
1 cup (4 ounces) grated Cheddar cheese
⅔ cup shortening or lard
5 tablespoons cold water

Filling:
6 cups (6 to 8 medium) peeled and sliced apples
2 teaspoons lemon juice
¾ cup sugar
2 tablespoons flour
½ teaspoon cinnamon
½ teaspoon nutmeg
⅛ teaspoon salt
¾ cup (4 or 5 squares) crushed graham crackers
1 cup (4 ounces) grated Cheddar cheese
2 tablespoons butter

Sift together flour and salt. Cut in cheese and shortening until pieces are pea-sized. Sprinkle water over mixture, 1 teaspoon at a time, mixing lightly with a fork after each addition. Add only enough water to hold pastry together. Work quickly. Do not overhandle.

Divide pastry into two balls. Flatten each on a lightly floured surface. Roll out ⅛ inch thick and 1 inch larger than the overall size of the plate. Roll entire crust over rolling pin. Unroll into pie plate, carefully fitting it to the plate so it is not stretched. Trim around edge of plate.

For filling, sprinkle lemon juice over apple slices. Toss with mixture of sugar, flour, cinnamon, nutmeg and salt.

Sprinkle cracker crumbs over bottom crust. Cover with one-third of apple mixture. Top with ½ cup cheese. Repeat apple and cheese layers, ending with apples. Heap last layer of apples in the center. Dot with butter.

Moisten edge of bottom pastry with water for a tight seal. Arrange top crust over filling. Press edges to seal. Fold extra top pastry under bottom pastry and flute edge. Cut slits in crust.

Bake at 450°F for 10 minutes. Reduce heat to 350°F and bake for 40 minutes, or until crust is lightly browned. Serve warm or at room temperature.

Chocolate Truffle Cake

This cake is very rich.

24 ounces semi-sweet chocolate chips
1 cup butter
6 eggs
1 tablespoon sugar
1 tablespoon flour

Melt chocolate and butter together in a double boiler over hot (not boiling) water. Do not overheat. Cool slightly. Beat together eggs and sugar for 10 minutes, or until light-colored and triple in volume. Sprinkle flour over beaten egg mixture and fold in. Gently fold into chocolate mixture.

Pour into a buttered 10-inch springform pan and bake at 375°F for 22 minutes. Do not overbake! Center should be soft. Cool to room temperature. Refrigerate 4 hours or overnight.

Excellent with raspberry sauce and whipped cream.

Serves 16.

Chocolate-Dipped Treats

1 pound Guittard bittersweet chocolate, or other high quality
    chocolate
Fruit (strawberries, cherries, dried fruit)
Nuts (almonds, pecans, peanuts, individually or in clusters)
Cookies (biscotti, butter cookies)
Hand-made candies

Break up chocolate and melt three-fourths of it in a double boiler over hot (not boiling) water, stirring constantly. Chocolate should not exceed 130°F. Add remaining chunks, one by one, stirring until melted. Dip fruits, nuts, cookies or candies to cover or partially cover; drain excess and place on a lightly buttered cookie sheet. Cool at room temperature.

Makes 90 candies.

Raspberry Spritzer

The surprising addition of vinegar tempers the sweetness and gives the drink a beautiful color.

For each serving, mix:

3 ounces sweet white wine
3 ounces club soda
2 teaspoons raspberry or blueberry vinegar

A non-alcoholic version is equally tasty. Substitute 3 ounces apple juice for the wine.

Polynesia, which means "many islands," includes Hawaii, New Zealand, Samoa, the Cook Islands and Easter Island. These far-flung islands vary in culture and cuisine, but there are many similarities. Straddling the equator, they share the warm waters of the Pacific and a tropical climate, ensuring a diet rich in fish and fruits. Polynesians usually don't allow food to become overly troublesome or complicated, but their cooking is still distinctive and delicious.

POLYNESIAN *LUAU*

Tropical Itch

Pupus (Appetizers)

Lomi Lomi Salmon   Skewered Shrimp

Hawaiian Chicken Wings

Oven Kalua Pig

Green Rice

Fresh Fruit Salad

Sweet Potato *Poi*

Macadamia Nut Chiffon Pie

Tropical Itch

Serve these with a backscratcher, then sit back and enjoy the sunset.

For each drink:

Juice of ½ lime
1 ounce rum
1 ounce Curaçao or other orange liqueur
Dash of bitters
Passion fruit juice

Mix lime juice, rum, Curaçao and bitters; pour over shaved ice in a tall glass. Fill with passion fruit juice and stir.

Lomi Lomi Salmon

1 pound frozen salmon, thawed
1 quart water
1 cup salt
5 ripe tomatoes, peeled
1 green pepper
4 green onions
1 tablespoon vinegar
Salt and pepper to taste

Soak salmon overnight in brine made from water and salt. Skin and cut salmon in ¼-inch cubes. Chop tomatoes, green pepper and onion. Mix with salmon. Stir in vinegar, salt and pepper. Refrigerate overnight.

Storing the raw fish for 48 hours in a deep-freeze kills parasites that may be present.

Skewered Shrimp

¾ cup soy sauce
½ cup pineapple juice
¼ cup rice vinegar
60 medium shrimp, unshelled

Combine soy sauce, pineapple juice and vinegar. Add shrimp and marinate in refrigerator overnight.

Thread 4 or 5 shrimp on a bamboo skewer (don't crowd them). Grill outdoors or broil in the oven for 5 or 6 minutes, turning once and basting with marinade.

Provide a container for shells and lots of napkins for guests.

Hawaiian Chicken Wings

½ cup flour
½ teaspoon salt
¼ teaspoon white pepper
2 pounds chicken wings, disjointed (2 meaty sections only)
2 tablespoons cooking oil
½ cup pineapple juice
2 tablespoons lemon juice
2 tablespoons soy sauce

Mix flour, salt and pepper in a paper bag. Add chicken and shake to coat. Brown quickly in oil. Combine pineapple juice, lemon juice and soy sauce. Pour over chicken. Cover tightly and simmer 30 minutes, or until chicken is tender.

Oven Kalua Pig

*In a traditional **luau**, an entire pig is roasted in a pit.*

10- to 12-pound pork loin roast or pork butt
½ cup coarse salt
1 teaspoon liquid smoke
6 or 7 *ti* or banana leaves

Rub salt on pork. Sprinkle with liquid smoke. Wrap in leaves and tie with string. Wrap in heavy foil and seal securely. Bake at 250°F for 7 hours, or until meat is "fall-apart" tender.

Fresh Fruit Salad

Toss together chunks of fresh fruit as available, such as pineapple, papaya, avocado, banana, orange, melon and strawberries. Add a little rum or grenadine, if desired. Serve on a bed of lettuce.

Green Rice

2 cups water
1 cup rice
½ teaspoon salt
½ cup butter
½ cup chopped onion
1 pound fresh spinach, stemmed and chopped
2 cups milk
2 eggs, beaten
1½ cups grated Cheddar cheese

Add rice and salt to boiling water. Cover, reduce heat and simmer 20 minutes, or until liquid is absorbed.

Saute onion in butter until soft. Add spinach and cook 2 minutes, or until limp. Stir spinach, milk, eggs and cheese into rice. Bake at 350°F for 45 minutes in a 2-quart casserole.

Sweet Potato *Poi*

*Proper **poi** is made from pounded taro root. This version is more adaptable to mainland kitchens. **Poi** is measured in consistency by how many fingers it takes to scoop up a mouthful. Thus, "two-finger **poi**" is thicker than "three-finger **poi**."*

8 sweet potatoes
¾ cup coconut milk
Salt and pepper to taste

Boil potatoes in their skins until tender. Peel and mash until smooth. Gradually beat in coconut milk. Add salt and pepper.

Macadamia Nut Chiffon Pie

2 eggs, separated
½ cup plus 2 tablespoons sugar, divided
Pinch of salt
2 cups milk, scalded
1 package (1 tablespoon) unflavored gelatin, softened in
¼ cup cold water
1 teaspoon vanilla
¼ cup ground macadamia nuts, divided
9-inch pie shell, baked
1 cup heavy cream, whipped with 1 tablespoon sugar

Whisk egg yolks with ¼ cup sugar and salt. Slowly stir in hot milk. Cook in a double boiler, stirring constantly, for 5 minutes, or until thickened; remove from heat. Add softened gelatin, stirring until dissolved. Cover and chill 1 hour, or until mixture begins to thicken.

Beat egg whites until stiff peaks form, gradually adding 6 tablespoons sugar. Fold into chilled custard with vanilla and ½ cup nuts. Pour into cool pie shell.

Top with whipped cream and sprinkle with remaining nuts. Chill until ready to serve.

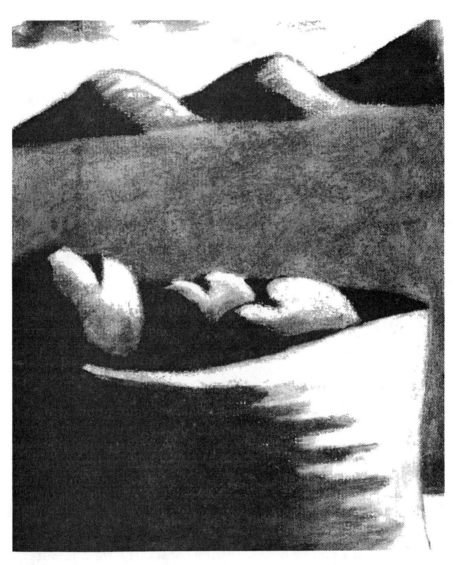

Scandinavian ingredients tend to be simple, since the small, rural communities do not have easy access to a wide variety of fruits, vegetables and spices.

Denmark is best known for its rich pastries and fine pork. Finland's hearty rye bread makes any mouth water. Norwegians and Swedes eat herring and a great variety of other fish in many forms at any time of day. The northern blueberries, lingonberries and cloudberries are creatively incorporated into their diets.

Dark, whole-grain breads and potatoes are consumed in large quantities all over Scandinavia. And we must not forget the warming "water of life," **aquavit** . . . served ice cold and drunk with ceremony and gusto!

SCANDINAVIA

Glögg
Swedish Mulled Wine

Gravlax
Salmon Cured with Dill

Blåbær Suppe
Norwegian Blueberry Soup

Mørbrad med Svedsker
Danish Prune-Stuffed Pork Roast

Jansson's Frestelse
Jansson's Temptation

Rødkål
Danish Braised Red Cabbage

Hiiavaleipa
Finnish Rye Bread

Äppelkaka
Swedish Apple Cake

Glögg
Swedish Mulled Wine

This will thaw the longest, darkest Scandinavian winter night!

1 bottle dry red wine (Burgundy or Zinfandel)
1 cup sweet vermouth
1 tablespoon Angostura bitters
1 cup raisins
Peel and juice of 1 orange
5 whole cloves
1-inch piece ginger root
1 stick cinnamon
1 cup aquavit
¾ cup sugar
1 cup blanched almonds
1 lemon, sliced

In a 5-quart nonreactive pot, mix wine, vermouth, bitters, raisins, orange peel and juice, cloves, ginger and cinnamon. Let stand overnight.

At serving time, bring mixture quickly to a boil. Remove from heat; stir in aquavit, sugar, almonds and lemon slices. Serve hot in mugs, accompanied by small spoons for scooping out the nuts and raisins.

Gravlax
Salmon Cured with Dill

3-pound salmon, filleted, but not skinned
½ cup sugar
½ cup coarse salt
1 bunch fresh dill

Sauce:
4 tablespoons dark, strong mustard
1 teaspoon powdered mustard
3 tablespoons sugar
2 tablespoons white vinegar
⅓ cup vegetable oil
3 tablespoons chopped fresh dill weed

Mix sugar and salt and liberally coat salmon on all sides. Place dill over one cut side and place halves together. Put salmon in a plastic bag large enough for fish to lie flat. Close bag tightly and place in a baking dish to catch drips. Set a weighted platter on top of salmon. Refrigerate 3 days, turning bag twice a day to marinate the fish in the liquid that is extracted. Replace the weighted platter each time.

For sauce, mix the mustards, sugar and vinegar to a paste. Whisk in oil until mixture thickens. Stir in dill. If sauce separates before using, whisk again.

When ready to serve, remove fish from marinade, scrape off dill and seasoning and pat dry. Place the fillets skin side down on a cutting board and slice diagonally, cutting each slice away from the skin. Accompany with Finnish Rye Bread (see page 160) and the mustard sauce.

Storing the raw fish for at least 48 hours in a deep-freeze kills parasites that may be present.

Blåbær Suppe
Norwegian Blueberry Soup

2 quarts blueberries
¼ cup lemon juice
2 cups sugar
6 tablespoons cornstarch
½ cup water
1 teaspoon cinnamon
½ teaspoon salt
1 cup sour cream

Simmer berries in water to cover for 10 minutes, or until soft. Strain through cheesecloth, as for jelly. Measure juice, adding water as needed to make 4 cups. Add lemon juice and sugar; reheat. Mix cornstarch with ½ cup water. Add to boiling juice with cinnamon and salt, stirring constantly until clear and slightly thickened; chill. Garnish with sour cream.

Mørbrad med Svedsker
Danish Prune-Stuffed Pork Roast

5-pound boneless pork loin roast
12 pitted prunes
1 teaspoon salt
2 teaspoons coarsely ground black pepper
2 large onions, thinly sliced
½ cup orange juice
¼ cup dry sherry
3 tablespoons vegetable oil
3 tablespoons grated ginger root
1 tablespoon cornstarch
¼ cup cold water
¼ cup cream
1 tablespoon currant jelly

With a long, sharp knife, poke a hole through the roast from one end to the other. With the handle of a wooden spoon, push the prunes into the slit, one at a time. Sprinkle salt and pepper evenly on all sides of roast.

Line a 9 × 13 × 2-inch baking pan with onions and set roast on top. Mix juice, sherry, oil and ginger; pour over roast. Basting occasionally with pan juices, roast at 350°F for 3 hours, or until meat thermometer reads 185°F.

Transfer roast and onions to a serving platter. Strain pan juices into a saucepan and reduce to 1 cup. Mix cornstarch with water. Over medium heat, whisk into sauce with cream and jelly. Cook until slightly thickened.

Jansson's Frestelse
Jansson's Temptation

4 tablespoons butter, divided
2 tablespoons oil
2 large onions, thinly sliced
7 medium potatoes, cut in strips 2 inches long and ¼ inch thick
16 flat anchovies, drained
White pepper to taste
2 tablespoons fine dry bread crumbs
½ cup milk
¼ cup heavy cream

Saute onions in oil and 2 tablespoons butter for 10 minutes, or until soft but not brown. In a greased 2-quart baking dish, arrange alternate layers of potatoes, onions and anchovies, ending with potatoes. Sprinkle each layer with a little pepper. Sprinkle bread crumbs over top and dot with remaining butter. Scald milk and cream; pour over potatoes. Bake at 350°F for 1 hour, or until potatoes are tender.

Rødkål
Danish Braised Red Cabbage

1 medium head red cabbage, cored
⅓ cup water
⅓ cup white vinegar
4 tablespoons butter
1 tablespoon sugar
1 teaspoon salt
¼ cup currant jelly
1 small apple, peeled and grated

Shred cabbage finely. In a 5-quart casserole, heat water, vinegar, butter, sugar and salt. Add cabbage and toss to coat. Cover tightly. Braise in a 350°F oven for 2 hours. Add a little water if it dries out. Ten minutes before serving, stir in jelly and apple. Serve hot.

The flavor improves if made a day ahead and refrigerated. Reheat to serve.

Hiiavaleipa
Finnish Rye Bread

3 cups rye flour
3 cups white flour
¼ cup sugar
1 tablespoon salt
1 package active dry yeast, undissolved
2 tablespoons butter, softened
2 cups very warm water (120° to 130°F)

Combine rye flour and 2 cups white flour. In a large, warm bowl, thoroughly mix 2 cups flour mixture, sugar, salt and yeast. Add butter and water and beat 2 minutes with mixer at medium speed. Add 1 cup flour mixture. Beat at high speed for 2 minutes. Stir in remaining flour mixture and enough white flour to make a soft dough. Cover and let rest 10 minutes. Knead until smooth and elastic. Place in a greased bowl, turning to grease surface. Cover and let rise 1 hour, or until double. Punch down. Shape dough into 2 balls. On greased baking sheets, flatten to 1-inch thickness. Cover and let rise 1 hour, or until double. Bake at 400°F for 25 to 30 minutes. Cool on racks.

Äppelkaka
Swedish Apple Cake

10 tablespoons unsalted butter, divided
3 cups dry bread crumbs
3 tablespoons sugar
1½ teaspoons cinnamon
2½ cups applesauce

Melt 8 tablespoons butter. Add bread crumbs, sugar and cinnamon; saute 5 minutes until mixture is lightly and evenly browned.

Butter a 2½-quart baking dish. Cover bottom with a ½-inch layer of crumbs. Spoon on a ½-inch layer of applesauce. Continue alternating layers, finishing with crumbs. Dot with remaining butter. Bake at 375°F for 25 minutes. Let cool and serve at room temperature.

Sephardic Jews were the scholars and bankers during the Moorish domination of the Iberian Peninsula ("Sepharad" is the Hebrew word for Spain). During the Inquisition, most fled to Turkey and the Isle of Rhodes. Their distinct cuisine incorporates tastes of southern Europe and the Middle East. The Sephardim often begin a meal with a toast: **Comé con gana** — eat with gusto!

SEPHARDIC BRUNCH

Bourikitas
Filled Turnovers

Huevos Haminados
Hard-Cooked Eggs, Sephardic-Style

Quajado de Espinaca
Spinach Soufflé

Karnabit
Cauliflower Casserole

Platter of Feta cheese cubes, Greek olives,
sliced tomatoes and cucumbers

Roska
Sephardic Bread

Minenas
Date Cookies

Raki Biscochos
Anise-Flavored Cookies

Cafe Turko
Turkish Coffee

Bourikitas
Filled Turnovers

Dough:

1 cup ice water
1 cup oil
2 teaspoons lemon juice
½ teaspoon salt
5 cups flour
2 tablespoons oil for brushing tops
4 tablespoons grated Parmesan cheese

Mix water, oil, lemon juice and salt. Stir in flour and knead to a firm dough. Shape into walnut-sized balls and allow to stand in refrigerator for 5 minutes. Roll balls out on a lightly floured board into 2-inch rounds. Fill each with 1 teaspoon filling, fold over to a semicircle and trim edges. Moisten edges with water and seal well. Brush tops with oil and sprinkle with cheese. Bake on a greased baking sheet at 400°F for 30 minutes until golden-brown. Best served hot.

Makes 80 to 100 *bourikitas*. Extras may be frozen, unbaked, and stored in covered container.

Potato-Cheese Filling:

2 medium potatoes, boiled and mashed
½ cup grated Cheddar cheese
¼ cup cottage cheese
1 egg, beaten
½ teaspoon salt

Mix all ingredients. If necessary, thin with some warm milk. Mixture should be thick and fluffy.

Eggplant-Tomato Filling:

2 tablespoons oil
1 small eggplant, peeled and diced
1 small onion, diced
14½-ounce can tomatoes

Saute eggplant and onion in oil. Add tomatoes. Simmer, uncovered, for 1 hour, or until dry, stirring occasionally to prevent sticking.

Meat Filling:

1 tablespoon oil
1 small onion, finely chopped
1 tomato, peeled, seeded and chopped
½ pound ground meat (lamb, veal or beef)
¼ cup rice
½ cup water
Salt and pepper to taste
1 tablespoon chopped parsley

Saute onion in oil until soft. Add tomato, meat, rice, water, salt and pepper. Simmer, covered, for 15 minutes, or until all liquid has been absorbed. Stir in chopped parsley; cool.

Huevos Haminados
Hard-Cooked Eggs, Sephardic-Style

10 eggs
Water to cover
Outer brown skins from 6 to 10 onions
2 tablespoons oil
1 teaspoon salt
1 teaspoon pepper

Place all ingredients in a 4-quart pan, being careful not to crack the eggs. Bring to a boil, lower heat, cover and simmer 3 to 6 hours, adding water as needed to keep eggs covered. The long, slow cooking produces a unique color, texture and flavor. The eggs may be made ahead and rewarmed in boiling water for 3 minutes at serving time. Peel and cut in half lengthwise. Serve warm.

*The Sephardim have strong feelings about eggs. They are not taken out of the house after dark, and they **must** be cut in half immediately after being shelled. Whole eggs are served only in connection with funerals.*

Quajado de Espinaca
Spinach Soufflé

2 pounds fresh spinach, stemmed and chopped
½ cup instant mashed potatoes
6 eggs, well beaten
1 cup grated Romano cheese
2 teaspoons salt
2 tablespoons oil

Mix spinach, potatoes, eggs, cheese and salt. Coat bottom of a 9 × 9-inch baking dish with oil and pour in batter. Bake, uncovered, at 350°F for 45 minutes, or until golden-brown. Cut in squares to serve.

Karnabit
Cauliflower Casserole

1 large head cauliflower
2 eggs, beaten
Flour to coat
Oil for frying
3 tablespoons oil
1 cup diced celery
1 cup diced potato
½ cup diced carrot
1 cup peeled and chopped tomatoes
Juice of 1 lemon
Salt and pepper to taste

Soak cauliflower, head down, in cold salted water for 20 minutes; drain. Separate florets and parboil 5 minutes in salted water to which 1 slice of bread has been added (to eliminate cooking odor). Rinse under cold water and drain. Coat florets with beaten egg, then flour; fry in ½ inch oil until golden. Set aside.

In a large skillet with a lid, saute celery, potato and carrot in 3 tablespoons oil. Add tomato, lower heat and simmer until tender, adding water as necessary. Stir in lemon juice, salt and pepper. Place cauliflower on vegetable base and simmer 15 minutes. Arrange in an ovenproof casserole; cover and bake at 325°F for 15 minutes.

Roska
Sephardic Bread

Dough:
2 packages yeast
1 teaspoon sugar
2½ cups warm water (120° to 130°F)
10 cups flour
3 eggs
¾ cup sugar
½ cup oil
¼ teaspoon cinnamon

Topping:
1 egg, beaten
2 tablespoons white sesame seeds

Mix yeast, sugar and 1 cup water; set aside. Put 8 cups flour into a mixing bowl. Make a well and add eggs, sugar, oil, cinnamon, yeast mixture and remaining water. Beat, adding more flour as needed to make a stiff dough. Knead until smooth and elastic. Let rise in a warm place for 1½ hours, or until doubled. Punch down and break off pieces of dough the size of an egg. Roll each piece into an 8-inch rope and tie in a loose knot. Let rise again 30 minutes, or until double. Place on a baking sheet lined with floured waxed paper. Brush with beaten egg and sprinkle with sesame seeds. Bake at 350°F for 20 to 30 minutes, or until golden.

Minenas
Date Cookies

1 cup butter, room temperature
½ cup powdered sugar, divided
1 teaspoon vanilla
4 cups flour
2 cups (12 ounces) pitted dates
¾ cup walnuts
1 tablespoon water
¼ teaspoon cloves

Cream butter, 3 tablespoons sugar and vanilla; blend in flour. Grind together dates, nuts, water and cloves.

Flour hands. Make a depression in a walnut-sized piece of dough and fill with ½ teaspoon date filling. Mold dough completely around filling and roll into an oblong. Prick top with a fork. Repeat until all dough and filling are used. Bake at 350°F for 30 minutes. When cool, sprinkle tops with remaining powdered sugar.

Raki Biscochos
Anise-Flavored Cookies

Raki *is the Turkish word for the anise-flavored grape brandy of the Middle East. Ouzo is more available here.*

1 egg white
1 cup sugar
1⅓ cups *raki* or *ouzo*, a Greek liqueur
½ cup oil
4½ teaspoons baking powder
3 to 4 cups flour
1 egg, beaten
1 tablespoon sesame seeds

Beat egg white with sugar; add *raki*, oil and baking powder mixed with 3 cups flour. Add more flour as needed to make a moderately firm dough. Let dough rest 5 minutes.

On a lightly floured board, divide dough into three parts. Roll each part into a cylinder 1 inch thick; cut each cylinder into 1-inch lengths. Roll each length into a 6-inch rope ¼ inch thick. Form into any of the following shapes:

1. Pinch 3 ropes together at one end and braid loosely. Pinch end to finish.

2. Bend each rope into a pretzel shape.

3. Tie the ends of a rope together to form a wreath.

Place on a greased cookie sheet. Brush with beaten egg and sprinkle with sesame seeds. Bake at 375°F for 20 minutes, or until lightly browned.

Cafe Turko
Turkish Coffee

This strong, sweet coffee is as much a gesture of hospitality as a beverage. In the Middle East, guests are often greeted with tiny cups containing just a few drops of coffee. It must be made with a very finely ground coffee, sometimes called Turkish grind.

1¾ cups water
3 heaping teaspoons Turkish grind coffee
3 heaping teaspoons sugar

Bring 1½ cups water to a boil. Remove from heat; stir in coffee and sugar. Bring just to a boil, remove from heat and add ¼ cup water. Bring to a boil a third time; remove from heat. Spoon a little foam into each demitasse cup before pouring coffee.
Serves 8.

The custom of **zakuski**, or appetizers, was introduced in 862 A.D. by Rurik, the Scandinavian prince who became the first czar of Russia. **Zakuski** are an important part of the meal. Enthusiastic toasts, **"Za vashe zdoróye"** (To your health), are followed by tiny glassfuls of vodka and small bites of **zakuski**.

SOVIET UNION

Zakuski (Appetizers)
Ikra
Russian Caviar Platter
Kõrvitsasalat
Estonian Pickled Pumpkin
Rosolje
Estonian Beet and Herring Salad
Citrinis Vodka
Lithuanian Lemon Vodka

Pirukad
Estonian Stuffed Pastries

Borsch
Russian Beet and Cabbage Soup

Tåidetud Vasikarind
Estonian Veal Shoulder Roast

Karabakh Loby
Azerbaijani Green Beans and Tomatoes

Paskha
Russian Easter Cheese Mold

Kulich
Russian Sourdough Easter Cake

Ikra
Russian Caviar Platter

Russians usually eat caviar alone on buttered white bread. This nontraditional presentation of caviar, with complementary condiments on cream cheese, is especially attractive and tasty.

6 hard-cooked eggs, peeled
8 ounces whipped cream cheese
1 ounce black caviar
6 green onions, finely chopped
4 ounces red caviar (salmon roe)
½ cup finely chopped parsley
8 slices white or rye bread

Cut eggs in half and remove yolks. Chop yolks and whites separately. Spread cream cheese smoothly on a 10-inch platter. Mound black caviar in center of cheese. Surround with concentric circles of chopped yolks, green onions, red caviar, chopped whites and parsley.

Cut each bread slice into four triangles. Bake on a cookie sheet at 450°F, turning once, until lightly toasted on both sides. Serve at once with small knives, so guests may spread their choice of toppings on toast.

Kõrvitsasalat
Estonian Pickled Pumpkin

*This relish is served with meat dishes as well as on the **zakuska** table.*

2 pounds pumpkin
¾ cup sugar
1 cup vinegar
1 stick cinnamon
2 whole cloves

Peel and seed pumpkin. Cube. Boil sugar and vinegar together for 5 minutes. Pour over pumpkin cubes, cover and let stand overnight.

Drain pumpkin cubes and strain liquid into a saucepan. Add cinnamon and cloves. Boil 5 minutes. Remove cinnamon and cloves; add pumpkin cubes. Boil until translucent. Let cool. Pack in a large covered jar. Pumpkin will keep refrigerated for several weeks.

Rosolje
Estonian Beet and Herring Salad

1 pound potatoes, boiled in the skin and peeled
1 pound beets, boiled in the skin and peeled
1 apple, cored
½ pound dill pickles
2 pickled herrings, or more to taste, finely diced
1 onion, finely chopped
1 pound leftover pot roast or ham, diced, optional
1 tablespoon dry mustard
1 tablespoon pickle juice
2 teaspoons sugar
1 cup yogurt or sour cream

Garnish:
3 hard-cooked eggs, finely chopped
Sliced dill pickle
Sprigs parsley

Dice potatoes, beets, apple and pickles. Mix with herring, onion and meat, if used. Mix mustard, pickle juice, sugar and yogurt. Stir into salad. Mound on serving plate and garnish with chopped eggs, sliced pickle and parsley.

*Meat is added to make the **Rosolje** a main course.*

Citrinis Vodka
Lithuanian Lemon Vodka

Peel of ½ lemon
1 bottle (fifth or quart) vodka, divided
4 lemons, quartered
2 cups sugar
1 cup water

Soak lemon peel in ½ cup vodka for 24 hours. Add lemons, sugar and water; simmer 15 minutes. Let cool. Strain. Add the remaining vodka and bottle. Serve chilled or on the rocks.

Pirukad
Estonian Stuffed Pastries

Dough:
½ cup butter
2½ cups flour
1 egg, lightly beaten
5 tablespoons sour cream

Filling:
1 tablespoon butter
1 onion, chopped
2 cups finely chopped pork or veal, uncooked
1 hard-cooked egg, diced
½ teaspoon salt
¼ teaspoon pepper

Egg wash:
1 egg, whisked with 1 tablespoon water

Cut butter into flour until it resembles coarse meal. Add egg and sour cream; mix well. Refrigerate dough for 1 hour.

Saute onion in butter. Combine with meat, diced egg, salt and pepper.

Roll out dough evenly to ¼-inch thickness. Cut into 3-inch circles. Place a tablespoon of filling in center of each circle and fold the dough over to cover the filling, forming a semi-circle. Moisten edges with water and pinch together. Brush top of pastries with egg wash. Bake at 350°F for 20 minutes, or until light brown.

Borsch
Russian Beet and Cabbage Soup

1 pound lean beef chuck, cut in small cubes
2 quarts water
1 teaspoon salt
2 tablespoons butter
2 cups peeled and grated raw beets
1 cup grated carrots
1 cup grated turnips
1 large onion, chopped
¼ cup tomato sauce
3 tablespoons vinegar
1½ teaspoons sugar
½ teaspoon freshly ground black pepper
2 bay leaves
1 small head cabbage, shredded
1 cup sour cream or yogurt

Simmer beef cubes, covered, in salted water for 1½ hours.

In a large pot, melt butter; add beets, carrots, turnips, onion, tomato sauce, vinegar, sugar, pepper and bay leaves. Cover and simmer 15 minutes, stirring frequently. Add cabbage and cook 10 minutes longer. Combine with meat and broth. Cook until vegetables are tender. Remove bay leaves. Taste for seasoning. Serve with sour cream to spoon into soup.

Tåidetud Vasikarind
Estonian Veal Shoulder Roast

1 pound ground lean veal or beef
½ pound ground lean pork
½ cup fresh bread crumbs
1 cup finely chopped onion
2 eggs, lightly beaten
1 teaspoon salt
1 teaspoon freshly ground black pepper
5-pound boned shoulder of veal
4 hard-cooked eggs, peeled
1½ to 2 cups cold water or chicken stock
½ cup sour cream

For stuffing, combine ground meats, bread crumbs, onion, beaten eggs, salt and pepper. Mix thoroughly.

Open out veal shoulder. Make small cuts so that it lies flat. Pound to a fairly uniform thickness.

Spread half the stuffing on the veal to within 2 inches of the edges. Lay the hard-cooked eggs in a row down the length of the stuffing; spread remaining stuffing over eggs. Bring one long side of the veal over the filling to the middle, and tuck in the two ends. Bring the other side over the filling, enclosing it snugly. Tie the rolled veal crosswise at 2-inch intervals, then lengthwise.

Place veal, seam-side down, in a roasting pan just large enough to hold it comfortably. Pour in 1½ cups water or stock and roast at 350°F for 2 hours, basting every 30 minutes with the pan juices. When meat is a deep golden-brown, transfer to a serving platter and cut off strings.

Bring pan juices to a boil over high heat, scraping loose any solids. If most of the liquid has cooked away, add remaining water or stock. Remove from heat and stir in sour cream, 1 tablespoon at a time. Taste for seasoning.

Slice the roll crosswise 1 inch thick, and arrange slices on a large heated platter. Moisten slices with a few tablespoons of sauce. Serve remaining sauce separately.

Karabakh Loby
Azerbaijani Green Beans and Tomatoes

2 pounds fresh green beans, trimmed
½ cup butter
4 cups thinly sliced onions
2 small green peppers, seeded and cut into ½-inch pieces
6 medium tomatoes, peeled, seeded and coarsely chopped
2 tablespoons finely chopped fresh basil, or 2 teaspoons dried
1 cup sour cream
½ teaspoon salt
¼ teaspoon freshly ground black pepper

Boil beans, uncovered, in lightly salted water for 8 minutes, or until crisp-tender. Drain and rinse under cold water. Set aside.

Saute onion and green pepper in butter, stirring occasionally, for 5 to 8 minutes, or until vegetables are tender but not brown. Stir in tomatoes and basil; boil rapidly until most of the pan juices have evaporated. Stir in beans and simmer 2 minutes.

Beat together sour cream, salt and black pepper. Stir into the vegetables. Serve at once.

Paskha
Russian Easter Cheese Mold

Make this festive dessert 2 or 3 days in advance.

2 pounds dry cottage cheese, divided
1 cup butter, room temperature
1 cup sour cream
1 cup whipping cream
4 egg yolks
2 cups sugar
2 teaspoons vanilla
1 cup mixed candied fruits, divided
½ cup finely chopped blanched almonds
⅓ cup whole blanched almonds, toasted

In a food processor, puree 1 pound cottage cheese until smooth. Add ½ cup butter and process until smooth. Transfer to a large bowl. Repeat with remaining cottage cheese and butter. Stir in sour cream.

Heat whipping cream in a double boiler until small bubbles form around the edge. Beat together egg yolks and sugar until thick. Continue beating while pouring hot cream in a thin stream. Return to double boiler and cook over hot water, stirring constantly until liquid thickens. (Too much heat will curdle it.) Add vanilla and ½ cup candied fruits. Cool quickly over ice water, stirring constantly until custard is cool. Combine with cheese mixture. Stir in chopped almonds.

Use a traditional Russian form to mold this dessert, or use a clean 2-quart clay flower pot with a hole in the bottom or a large colander. Set the mold in a shallow bowl and line with several thicknesses of cheesecloth large enough to hang over the rim. Pour in the cheese custard and fold edges of cheesecloth lightly over the top. Press it with a weighted plate. Refrigerate 2 days, or until firm.

To unmold, unwrap cheesecloth from the top, invert a flat serving plate on top of the mold and, grasping the two firmly together, invert. Gently peel off the cheesecloth and decorate the *paskha* with ½ cup candied fruit and whole almonds.

Slice and serve alone, or spread thickly on slices of sourdough *Kulich* (see following recipe).

Paskha can be kept refrigerated for at least one week before serving. Rubbing the cottage cheese through a sieve is the traditional, and time-consuming, method of making it smooth.

Kulich
Russian Sourdough Easter Cake

1½ cups sourdough starter (available in gourmet shops and
    kitchen stores)
¼ cup sugar
1 teaspoon salt
2 tablespoons butter, melted
1 egg
⅓ cup chopped raisins
¼ cup chopped almonds
1 teaspoon grated lemon peel
3 cups flour

Frosting:
¾ cup powdered sugar
2 teaspoons lemon juice
1 to 2 teaspoons milk

Combine starter, sugar, salt and butter in a warm bowl. Stir in egg, raisins, almonds and lemon peel; beat vigorously for 1 minute. Beat in 2½ cups flour and turn out onto a floured board. Knead in enough additional flour to make a smooth and elastic dough. Let rise in a warm place for 2 to 3 hours, or until double.

Punch down and let rest 15 minutes. Place in a well-greased 3-pound coffee can. Cover and let rise in a warm place for 1½ to 2 hours, or until double.

Bake at 350°F for 45 minutes, or until well browned. Remove from can at once and cool on a rack.

Mix powdered sugar and lemon juice; gradually add milk until thick and smooth. Frost cooled *kulich*.

*Spanish foods are flavored by olive oil, garlic and onions, often with the addition of tomatoes and sweet peppers. This main meal would traditionally be eaten in the early afternoon, followed by a siesta. A Spaniard might break for sweets at five, then eat lightly (**tapas** in the bar or a soup at home) at ten o'clock.*

SPAIN

Sangría
Wine Punch

Sardinas en Cazuela
Sardines in Casserole

Delicias de Queso
Cheese Delights

Gazpacho a la Catalana
Catalan Chilled Vegetable Soup

Rapsodia de Mariscos
Seafood Rhapsody

Berenjenas Caserta
Eggplant Casserole

Ensalada Valenciana
Salad Valencia-Style

Brazo de Gitano
Andalusian Cake Roll

Sangría
Wine Punch

1 lemon, sliced ¼ inch thick
1 orange, sliced ¼ inch thick
½ to ¾ cup sugar
2 bottles (fifths) dry red wine
2 tablespoons brandy, optional
2 quarts club soda, chilled

Combine lemon and orange slices with sugar and put in a 3-quart pitcher. Pour in wine and brandy. Chill 2 hours or more. Just before serving, add club soda.

Makes 3 quarts.

White wine may be substituted for the red, and fruits such as peaches, nectarines or grapes may be substituted for the citrus.

Sardinas en Cazuela
Sardines in Casserole

3 cans sardines
½ cup extra virgin olive oil
3 large sweet onions, chopped
6-ounce can pimientos, cut in strips
Salt to taste

Rinse sardines quickly under warm water; drain. Pour half the olive oil over the bottom of a shallow casserole. Place a layer of chopped onions over the oil, then arrange sardines and pimiento over the onion. Cover with remaining oil. Bake at 350°F for 30 minutes. Serve hot from the casserole with forks and crusty French bread to scoop up the sauce.

Delicias de Queso
Cheese Delights

½ pound Parmesan cheese, grated
1 cup flour
5 tablespoons butter, room temperature
1 cup fine dry bread crumbs

Blend cheese with flour and butter. Form into small balls; roll in bread crumbs. Place on baking sheet. (These can be made several hours in advance and refrigerated.)

Bake at 350°F for 15 minutes, or until golden, turning once. Serve hot.

Makes 30.

Gazpacho a la Catalana
Catalan Chilled Vegetable Soup

4 cups chopped ripe tomatoes, divided
1 red or sweet white onion, peeled and chopped
2 cups peeled and chopped cucumber, divided
1½ cups seeded and chopped green bell pepper, divided
1½ cups soft bread crumbs
2 cloves garlic, minced
1 quart ice water
½ cup extra virgin olive oil
¼ cup wine vinegar
1 tablespoon paprika
1 teaspoon salt
½ cup chopped black olives
1 cup croutons

In a food processor or blender, puree 3½ cups tomato, onion, 1½ cups cucumber, 1 cup pepper, bread crumbs and garlic. Pour into a large bowl; beat in water, oil, vinegar, paprika and salt.

Cover and chill several hours. Stir in ½ cup each tomatoes, cucumber, pepper and olives. Sprinkle croutons on top. Serve very cold.

Rapsodia de Mariscos
Seafood Rhapsody

2 pounds fillet of sole
12 tablespoons butter, divided
1 pound small mushroom caps
⅓ cup minced onion
2 ripe tomatoes, peeled and chopped
¼ cup flour
1 quart half-and-half or milk
1 pound shelled, cooked shrimp
½ cup fine bread crumbs
1 tablespoon olive oil

Cut fish in 2-inch squares; saute lightly in 6 tablespoons butter for 3 to 5 minutes, or until opaque. Transfer to a 3-quart casserole.

Add remaining butter to pan; saute mushrooms and onion. When onion is tender, add tomatoes and cook 2 minutes; stir in flour. Slowly add half-and-half, stirring constantly, cooking until smooth. Add shrimp. Taste for seasoning.

Add to fish in casserole. Moisten crumbs with oil and sprinkle on top. Bake at 350°F for 20 minutes, or until crumbs are golden.

Berenjenas Caserta
Eggplant Casserole

2 pounds eggplant, thinly sliced
¾ cup olive oil, divided
2-ounce tin anchovy fillets, or ½ teaspoon anchovy paste
¾ cup fine dry bread crumbs, divided
2 medium tomatoes, peeled and chopped
1½ tablespoons grated Parmesan cheese
2 cloves garlic, minced
1½ tablespoons minced parsley
1½ tablespoons wine vinegar

Soak eggplant slices in salt water for 30 minutes; drain and dry. Saute in ⅔ cup oil until lightly browned; drain on paper towels.

Rinse anchovies under warm water; chop finely. Combine with ½ cup crumbs, tomato, cheese, garlic, parsley and vinegar.

Alternate tomato mixture and eggplant slices in layers in a 2½-quart casserole. Mix remaining ¼ cup crumbs with remaining oil. Sprinkle on top. Bake uncovered at 350°F for 1 hour.

Ensalada Valenciana
Salad Valencia-Style

4 oranges, peeled and thinly sliced
1 large red onion, thinly sliced
½ cup extra virgin olive oil
¼ cup red wine vinegar
¼ teaspoon salt
¼ teaspoon freshly ground black pepper
1 bunch salad greens, torn

Marinate oranges and onion in olive oil, vinegar, salt and pepper for 30 minutes. Toss with salad greens.

Brazo de Gitano
Andalusian Cake Roll

This 15-inch long "Gypsy's Arm" may have originally been decorated to resemble a woman's braceleted arm.

Cake Roll:
6 egg whites
4 egg yolks
¾ cup granulated sugar
⅛ teaspoon salt
½ cup sifted flour
3 tablespoons powdered sugar

Line a greased 10 × 15-inch jelly roll pan with waxed paper. Lightly grease and flour the paper. Preheat oven to 400°F. Beat egg whites until stiff; set aside. Beat egg yolks, granulated sugar and salt until thick and lemon-colored. Stir in flour until smooth. Add whites to batter one-third at a time, folding gently but thoroughly to remove air bubbles. Pour batter into pan, spreading evenly. Bake 10 to 15 minutes, or until cake springs back when touched. Loosen around edges with spatula; immediately invert cake onto waxed paper sprinkled with powdered sugar, and peel off waxed paper from top. Starting with a long edge, gently roll up and set aside.

Rum Custard Filling:
2 cups milk
1 vanilla bean, cut in pieces
2 egg yolks
¼ cup sugar
¼ cup flour
2 tablespoons dark rum
1 tablespoon butter

Scald milk with vanilla bean. Cover and remove from heat. Beat egg yolks and sugar until thick. Beat in flour, 1 tablespoon at a time. Remove vanilla bean and pour hot milk gradually into egg mixture, stirring constantly. Pour back into pan and continue to stir while cooking over low heat until mixture thickens, about 20 minutes. Stir in rum and butter. Cool to room temperature.

To assemble cake, unroll and spread filling evenly over top. Roll up and place on a serving plate, seam side down. Just before serving, sprinkle liberally with powdered sugar.

INDEX

I'd like to support the University of Washington Faculty Auxiliary Scholarship Fund. Please send me _____ additional copies of:

Cooking with All Your Faculties

Menus from Around the World
with the Faculty Auxiliary
of the University of Washington

Name _____

Address _____

City, State, Zip _____

_____ copies @ $12.95 each _____

Washington residents add 8.1% sales tax _____

Shipping and handling $2.00 per order

TOTAL _____

Send this form with remittance payable to Faculty Auxiliary to:

University of Washington Faculty Auxiliary
c/o Sue Christian
P.O. Box 26
Medina, WA 98039-0026